In these books you will find explorers, farmers, cowboys, heroes, villains, inventors, presidents, poets, pirates, artists, slaves, teachers, revolutionaries, priests, musicians— the girls and boys, men and women, who all became Americans....

OXFORD
A HISTORY OF
US

BOOK SEVEN

TEACHING GUIDE FOR

Reconstruction and Reform

1865–1890

Oxford University Press
New York

Oxford University Press

Oxford   New York
Athens Auckland Bangkok Bogotá Bombay
Buenos Aires Calcutta Cape Town Dar es Salaam Delhi
Florence Hong Kong Istanbul Karachi
Kuala Lumpur Madras Madrid Melbourne
Mexico City Nairobi Paris Singapore
Taipei Tokyo Toronto Warsaw
and associated companies in
Berlin   Ibadan

Editorial Development: Susan Washburn Buckley
Writer: Deborah Parks
Design: Nieshoff Design

ISBN 0-19-511093-5

3 5 7 9 8 6 4

Printed in the United States of America
on acid-free paper

Contents

A Note from the Author   4

About the Teaching Guide   6

Background for the Teacher   7

    Historical Overview   7

    Additional Resources   9

Teaching Strategies for Book Seven   10

    Introducing Book Seven   10

    Part 1: The Agony of Reconstruction (Chapters 1–7) 12

    Part 2: Retreat from the South (Chapters 8–10)   19

    Part 3: Battle for the West (Chapters 11–18)   23

    Part 4: Schemers and Dreamers (Chapters 19–21)   30

    Part 5: In Search of Liberty (Chapters 22–28)   34

    Part 6: Toward a New Century (Chapters 29–31)   40

    Part 7: The Unfinished Journey (Chapters 32–37)   43

    Summarizing Book Seven   48

Study Guides   50

    Part 1: The Agony of Reconstruction   50

    Part 2: Retreat from the South   51

    Part 3: Battle for the West   52

    Part 4: Schemers and Dreamers   53

    Part 5: In Search of Liberty   54

    Part 6: Toward a New Century   55

    Part 7: The Unfinished Journey   56

Note from the Author

Dear Teacher,

It is through story that people have traditionally passed on their ideas, their values, and their heritage. In recent years, however, we have come to think of stories as the property of the youngest of our children. How foolish of us. The rejection of story has made history seem dull. It has turned it into a litany of facts and dates. Stories make the past understandable (as well as enjoyable). Stories tell us who we are and where we've been. Without knowledge of our past, we can't make sense of the present.

As a former teacher, I knew of the need for a narrative history for young people, so I sat down and wrote one. (It took me seven years.) I was tired of seeing children struggle with arm-breaking, expensive books. I wanted my books to be inexpensive, light in weight, and user-friendly. Thanks to creative partnering by American Historical Publications and Oxford University Press, that's the way they are.

Called *A History of US*, mine is a set of 10 books. My hope is that they will help make American history—our story—a favorite subject again. It is important that it be so. As we prepare for the twenty-first century, we are becoming an increasingly diverse people. While we need to celebrate and enjoy that diversity, we also need to find solid ground to stand on together. Our history can provide that commonality. We are a nation built on ideas, on great documents, on individual achievement—and none of that is the property of any one group of us. Harriet Tubman, Abraham Lincoln, Emily Dickinson, Sequoya, and Duke Ellington belong to all of us—and so do our horse thieves, slave owners, and robber barons. We need to consider them all.

Now, to be specific, what do I intend these books to do in your classrooms? First of all, I want to help turn your students into avid readers. I want them to understand that nonfiction can be as exciting as fiction. (Besides, it is the kind of reading they'll meet most in the adult world.) I want to stretch their minds. I've written stories, but the stories are true stories. In nonfiction you grapple with the real world. I want to help children understand how fascinating that process can be.

I've tried to design books that I would have liked as a teacher— books that are flexible, easy-to-read, challenging, and idea-centered, that will lead children into energetic discussions. History can do that. It involves issues we still argue about. It gives us material with which to make judgments. It allows for comparisons. It hones the mind.

People all over this globe are dying—literally—because they want to live under a democracy. We've got the world's model and most of us don't understand or appreciate it. I want to help children learn about their country so they will be intelligent citizens. I want them to understand the heritage that they share with all the diverse people who are us—the citizens of the United States.

For some of your students, these books may be an introduction to history. What they actually remember will be up to you. Books can inspire and excite, but understanding big ideas and remembering details takes some reinforced learning. You'll find many suggestions for that in this Teaching Guide.

What you do with *A History of US* and this Teaching Guide will depend, of course, on you and your class. You may have students read every chapter or only some chapters, many volumes or only a few. (But, naturally, I hope they'll read it all. Our history makes good reading.) I hope you'll use the books to teach reading and thinking skills as well as history and geography. We need to stop thinking of subjects as separate from each other. We talk about integrating the curriculum; we need to really do it. History, broadly, is the story of a culture—and that embraces art, music, science, mathematics, and literature. (You'll find some of all of those in these books.)

Reading *A History of US* is easy; even young children seem to enjoy it. But some of the concepts in the books are not easy. They can be challenging to adults, which means that the volumes can be read on several levels. The idea is to get students excited by history and stretched mentally—at whatever their level of understanding. (Don't worry if every student doesn't understand every word. We adults don't expect that of our reading; we should allow for the same variety of comprehension among student readers.)

This Teaching Guide is filled with ideas meant to take the students back to the text to do a careful, searching read. It will also send them out to do research and writing and discovering on their own. The more you involve your students, the more they will understand and retain. Confucius, one of the world's great teachers, had this to say:

Tell me and I will forget. Show me and I will remember. Involve me and I will understand.

History is about discovering. It is a voyage that you and your students can embark on together. I wish you good sailing.

Joy Hakim

About the Teaching Guide

Like *A History of US*, this Teaching Guide is designed as a flexible resource to be used with students at varying levels. The guide for each volume presents teaching strategies, conceptual frameworks, and assessment suggestions as well as a range of activities for enrichment and extension. You will find the following sections in the Guide.

Background for the Teacher

A *Historical Overview* gives you a broad context for the stories and ideas presented in this volume of *A History of US*.

A list of *Additional Resources* offers brief descriptions of software, films, and videos for classroom use.

Teaching Strategies

Introducing Book Seven has suggestions for presenting the book's conceptual underpinnings, strategies for setting a geographical and chronological context for students, and a range of ongoing projects.

We have divided this volume (and every volume) of *A History of US* into Parts whose chapters have a common theme or focus. The Teaching Strategies for the Parts are as follows.

- *The Big Ideas* describes the underlying themes of the Part,
- *Chapter Summaries* gives a brief description of the content and list the key people, places, and terms in each chapter.
- *Introducing the Part* suggests ways to set a context in space and time. And by setting a context for reading, you can give students a framework of ideas for understanding the reading.
- *Discussing the Part* offers comprehension questions for Understanding the Chapters, activities for Making Connections between chapters or parts, and topics for Debating the Issues. Finally, students are involved in Making Ethical Judgments.
- The *Projects and Activities* for each part are varied by discipline, modality, and developmental level.
- *Bridging the Parts* gives links to other parts or volumes.

Summarizing Book Seven has suggestions for Discussing the Big Ideas, helping students synthesize what they have learned. Suggestions for Assessment includes strategies for both traditional and portfolio assessment.

Study Guides

At the end of each Teaching Guide are blackline masters that may be used as guides for independent reading or as tests for the Parts.

Background for the Teacher

Historical Overview

All persons born or naturalized in the United States, and subject to the jurisdiction thereof, are citizens of the United States and of the State wherein they reside. No State shall make or enforce any law which shall abridge the privileges or immunities of citizens of the United States; nor shall any State deprive any person of life, liberty, or property, without due process of law; nor deny to any person within its jurisdiction the equal protection of the laws.

—The Constitution of the United States, 14th Amendment, Section 1

Adopted in 1868, the 14th Amendment symbolized the best of Reconstruction—the urge to extend justice to all Americans. But passage of the Amendment did not come without a fight. President Andrew Johnson attacked it; twelve southern and border states rejected it. Resistance to the 14th Amendment handed control of Reconstruction to the Radical Republicans. Firebrands such as Thaddeus Stephens in the House and Charles Sumner in the Senate vowed to reshape southern society. In 1867, federal troops marched into the South and initiated Military Reconstruction. For southern states, the price of readmission to the Union became ratification of the 14th Amendment.

In 1869, in a further effort to write democratic principles and color blindness into the Constitution, the Radicals succeeded in pushing through the 15th Amendment for ratification. This measure forbade states to deny the right to vote "on account of race, color, or previous condition of servitude." Armed with the vote and backed by federal troops, African Americans won election to political offices at the local, state, and national levels for the first time in the nation's history. But their victories proved short-lived.

The moral fervor of the war and the passions of Reconstruction left the nation exhausted. When the southern states completed their march back into the Union, the North turned its attention to other matters. Amid the fury of a white backlash, African Americans found themselves the target of pent-up anger over Military Reconstruction. Therefore, although Reconstruction had proclaimed anew the American principle of human equality, it failed to secure it in reality. The South fell back into the hands of white Southerners and a new racial tyranny named Jim Crow.

In the closing years of the century, the pace of life quickened. Pioneers spilled pell-mell across the Mississippi. Cattle kings and sodbusters battled Native Americans for their last homeland. Railroad crews blasted through mountains and laid track across the Plains. Meanwhile, immigrants poured into the United States by the millions. In assessing the period, economist and social reformer Henry George remarked:

There is in all the past nothing to compare with the rapid changes now going on. . . . The snail's pace of crawling ages has suddenly become the headlong rush of the locomotive.

When the United States celebrated its one hundredth birthday in 1876, most Americans welcomed the chance to focus on the marvels of progress rather than the agonies of Reconstruction. They celebrated American inventiveness in a grand Centennial Exposition held in Philadelphia. For six months, some ten million people strolled through Machinery Hall to glimpse the start of the industrial age. But the Centennial Exposition showed only one side of American life. It concealed the unresolved issue of equality. The sight of Susan B. Anthony reading the Declaration of Sentiments at the Woman's Building hinted at the lack of rights for women. But few people paid any attention to Anthony—women's suffrage belonged to the next century. Even less attention was paid to the lack of rights for Native Americans and the African Americans who staggered under the heavy hand of the institutionalized segregation called Jim Crow. The glaring gaps between the rich and poor were also absent from the fair. Most of the poor could barely afford to eat, much less buy a ticket to attend the Exposition.

The growing pains of rapid change could be felt all across the continent—in the West where Native Americans lost their land, on the Pacific Coast where Asian immigrants felt the sting of prejudice, in the South where blacks and whites tried to build a "New South," in the East and Midwest where immigrants swelled the cities and fueled new industries with their labor. Guiding the nation through this period of turmoil were the same principles that had guided it through the trauma of its revolutionary birth. Americans still clung to the ideals proclaimed by the Declaration of Independence. So did the millions of immigrants who came to the United States in pursuit of these ideals. It was these beliefs that united the nation's diverse people and directed their search for perfection. Declared civil rights' defender W.E.B. DuBois:

We are Americans, not only by birth and by citizenship, but by our political ideals. . . . And the greatest of those ideals is that ALL MEN [AND WOMEN] ARE CREATED EQUAL.

Book Seven traces the passage of the United States into the modern era and its second century of existence as a "government of the people, by the people, and for the people." Each of the seven parts recommended for teaching the book serves as a "roadmarker" on the journey. The titles for these parts are as follows.

Part 1: The Agony of Reconstruction (Chapters 1–7)
Part 2: Retreat from the South (Chapters 8–10)
Part 3: Battle for the West (Chapters 11–18)
Part 4: Schemers and Dreamers (Chapters 19–21)
Part 5: In Search of Liberty (Chapters 22–28)
Part 6: Toward a New Century (Chapters 29–31)
Part 7: The Unfinished Journey (Chapters 32–37)

Explanation of each of these parts and suggestions for teaching can be found on pages 10–49.

Additional Resources for the Classroom

CD-Rom

The American Indian: A Multimedia Encyclopedia, Facts on File. (Uses text, images, and sound to tell the story of the Native Americans. A good source of information on the Plains peoples)

Laser Disks

The 1880s, Kaw Valley Films. (Gives students a glimpse into what life was like over a century ago)

How the West Was Lost, Discovery Channel. (Artifacts, interviews, photographs, and film footage tell the story of westward expansion from a Native American perspective.)

Sarah, Plain and Tall, Hallmark Hall of Fame. (Adaptation of the Newbery Award-winning children's book of the travels of a woman from Maine onto the prairie as a mail-order bride)

Software

American Inventions, Social Studies School Services. (A simulation in which students help extraterrestrials solve problems by searching through a catalog of American inventions)

Civil War and Reconstruction, Mindscape. (Helps guide student inquiry through the use of graphics and research-based questions)

Ellis Island, Educational Activities. (Takes students back to 1892 where they take on the identities of several Italian teenagers headed to America)

Golden Spike, National Geographic. (Involves students in the competition to complete the nation's first transcontinental railroad)

The War on the Indians, Focus Media. (Develops empathy by placing students in the role of a United States cavalry member or a Native American)

Filmstrips

Black History in America, Part 2, Educational Design. (Focuses on the late nineteenth century, from the end of Reconstruction to the start of the Niagara Movement)

A Last Frontier, Multi-Media Productions. (Debunks myths about the character of the "Wild West")

Videos

The Adventures of Huckleberry Finn, MGM. (Mark Twain's classic tale)

The Black West, All Media Productions. (Tells the story of the black pioneers who headed west)

Homesteading, United Learning. (Covers the settlement of the Great Plains during the years 1862–1932)

The Immigrant Experience, Social Studies School Services. (The story of a young Polish girl—Joan Micklin Silver—who immigrates to the U.S.)

Mark Twain, Coronet. (A fourteen-minute profile of Samuel Langhorne Clemens from boyhood to author)

The Railroad Builders, Encyclopaedia Brittanica. (Captures the competition between the immigrant crews who worked on the Union Pacific and the Central Pacific, and the Native Americans who tried to stop them)

Introducing Book Seven

■ INTRODUCING THE BIG IDEAS

Book Seven explores three Big Ideas: **change, justice,** and **diversity.** These three ideas provide the thread that weaves together the 37 chapters in this volume of *A History of US*.

Introducing your students to these concepts at the beginning will help them put together the pieces of the puzzle to make sense of the past. One starting point might be to write the title of this book on the chalkboard—*Reconstruction and Reform.* Pointing out that the prefix re means "again" or "anew," help students decode the two key words in the title: re-construction = re-build; re-form = re-shape. Discuss the implications of change in these two words.

Now challenge students to think of things that might need rebuilding or reshaping in years following the Civil War. (You may want students to "re-view" the closing chapters in Book Six.) Lead students to understand that the nation still had to grapple with extending justice to those who had been enslaved. It also had to find a just policy for dealing with the South.

To introduce the concept of diversity, have students move past the title and into the Table of Contents. Ask them which chapter titles show that the United States was becoming more diverse geographically. Which titles show that it was becoming more diverse culturally? You might link the concepts of diversity and justice by asking students to consider what might happen to the United States if equal justice were not extended to all its diverse peoples. Would the democracy continue to work? Why or why not?

■ SETTING THE CONTEXT

You might set the stage for Book Seven by reading aloud the selection from the 14th Amendment on page 7 of this Guide. Your students may have read about the 14th Amendment in Book Six, but tell them that the story of the 14th Amendment still isn't finished. In fact, it forms an important part of all of Book Seven. Then read aloud the titles of the Parts in Book Seven (see the Table of Contents for this Guide). Do students think the story of the 14th Amendment is concluded in this book? Why or why not? (No, because the title of Part 7 is "The Unfinished Journey.")

To set the stage for Book Seven and the ongoing search for justice, have students read the Preface on pages 9–11. Be prepared for some debate. The Preface asks students to think ethically about some controversial issues such as capital punishment and abortion. Although you won't resolve these issues in class, you may want to allow students to argue about them. Use the arguments to show that the debate over the meaning of justice—i.e., the 14th Amendment's "due process of law"—is still going on in the present.

■ ONGOING PROJECTS

The following activities bridge the seven parts of Book Seven.

Using Parallel Time Lines Author Joy Hakim advises that a sense of chronology—rather than memorized dates—is what matters for students. Various kinds of time lines are invaluable aids in building this understanding of historical sequence.

Book Seven covers Reconstruction and the rise of Jim Crow in the South. It also looks at events happening elsewhere in the nation. To help students synthesize these two sets of events, you might have them construct parallel time lines. One time line should plot events that happened in or mainly affected the South. The other time line should plot events in the rest of the nation. Some items may appear on both time lines. Examples include passage of the 13th, 14th, and 15th amendments. Suggest that students use the Chronology on page 184 to determine the intervals (ten-year segments? twenty-year segments?) best suited for both time lines.

Students may want to write each item on a card to be attached to one of two clotheslines that face each other. In this way, students can pivot to see what's happening in the South and in the rest of the nation.

Using Maps Book Seven talks a lot about the movements of people. People head in and out of the South. They also spill across the Great Plains. At the same time, immigrants are arriving on both the West and East coasts. To follow these movements, have students use an opaque projector to create a large outline map on the chalkboard or on pieces of posterboard. At the end of each chapter or part, allow time for volunteers to locate and plot key movements on the class map. Encourage students to determine which of these movements increased the diversity of our nation. Which, if any, of the movements contributed to unity? (Immigration is a good example of movement that increased diversity, while movement of people by transcontinental railroads promoted unity.)

Writing History The author wants students to "shake up" the past. She hopes students will bring history alive by retelling and adding their own stories to *A History of US.* One way to accomplish this is to ask students to set up a separate section in their notebooks or three-ring binders in which they write their own history books.

When you finish each chapter, give students time to write their own accounts of events. (Students may want to dig deeper into the past or illustrate their histories.) Point out that Joy Hakim often suggests ideas for further investigation right in the book. From time to time, call on volunteers to share their histories with the class.

Teaching History Assign teams of students to work cooperatively to teach portions of the book. Remind students that the best teaching and learning occurs when everyone is involved. Students should think beyond lectures. Encourage them to enrich instruction with pictures, poems, art, and so on. The "teachers" should also devise short homework assignments or in-class activities. At the end of the lesson, they should submit several questions to be used as part of a self-evaluation test. (See Suggestions for Assessment on page 49.)

Making Class Reference Books Encourage students to create their own class references by compiling one or all of three helpful references: a class dictionary, a biographical dictionary, and/or a gazetteer. You might set up big notebooks arranged alphabetically in the front of the room. Every time a student learns a new word, discovers a new place, or finds an interesting or courageous actor in history, he or she should record the discovery in the appropriate reference. A short definition/description and appropriate illustration should be added. (Caution students to leave a lot of space between entries so that they can be recorded in alphabetical order. In fact, you might want to adopt a one-entry-per-page rule.)

PART 1
The Agony of Reconstruction (Chapters 1–7)

The Big Ideas

On January 3, 1867, Thaddeus Stevens, one of the leaders of the Radical Republicans, stood to address the House of Representatives. Declared Stevens:

Have not loyal blacks quite as good a right to choose rulers and make laws as rebel whites? . . . . I am for Negro suffrage in every rebel State. If it be just, it should not be denied; if it be necessary, it should be adopted; if it be a punishment to traitors, they deserve it.

Stevens felt the federal government should exert its full authority to ensure justice for former slaves. In Stevens's mind, this would never occur so long as any state could deny an individual "due process of law." He insisted that readmission of southern states to the Union hinge upon ratification of the 14th Amendment. Part 1 explores how this demand changed the course of Reconstruction—and opened the door for far-reaching changes in the civil rights of all Americans.

Chapter Summaries

Each of the seven chapters in Part 1 traces the painful process of healing a nation torn by civil war. Stories are as follows.

Chapter 1
Reconstruction Means Rebuilding (pp. 12–14)

The Civil War destroyed a way of life in the South. President Lincoln had hoped to reconstruct the region with a gentle hand. But his assassination deprived the nation of the patience and wisdom needed to heal its deep spiritual wounds.

People to Meet President Lincoln, Mark Twain, General Sherman

Place to Visit Charleston

Terms to Define polyglot, Reconstruction

Chapter 2
Who Was Andrew Johnson? (pp. 15–16)

Andrew Johnson had shown courage when he turned his back on sectionalism and chose loyalty to the Union instead. But when a bullet thrust Johnson into the presidency, a stubborn, uncompromising nature proved his undoing.

People to Meet Andrew Johnson, William Seward

Places to Visit Greeneville (in Tennessee), Alaska

Chapter 3
Presidential Reconstruction (pp. 17–20)

The Freedmen's Bureau attempted to help African Americans adjust to their new lives. But the passage of black codes and appearance of white supremacy groups such as the Ku Klux Klan threatened to undermine the justice for which the war had been fought.

People to Meet William Henry Johnson, Francis Porter, Edward Garrison Walker, George Lewis Ruffin, Mary Peake, General Lee, Jefferson Davis, Millie Freeman, General Philip Sheridan, Alexander Stephens, Charlotte Forten, Harriet Tubman, Reverend Francis J. Grimke

Places to Visit Hampton (in Virginia), Lynchburg (in Virginia), Memphis (in Tennessee), New Orleans, Port Royal (in South Carolina)

Terms to Define Presidential Reconstruction, Freedmen's Bureau, animosity, martial law, black codes

Chapter 4
Slavery and States' Rights (pp. 21–23)

Two amendments wiped out the causes of the Civil War. The 13th Amendment abolished slavery, and the 14th Amendment diluted states' rights. With passage of the 14th Amendment, the federal government became the guardian of individual liberty.

People to Meet Andrew Johnson, Charlotte Brown

Terms to Define unalienable (inalienable), radical, nullify, veto, Radical Republicans, states' rights

Chapter 5
Congressional Reconstruction (pp. 24–27)

In 1867, Radical Republicans in Congress wrested control of Reconstruction from the hands of the president. Once again, federal troops marched South. This time, they opened up the doors of government to newly enfranchised blacks.

People to Meet James Longstreet, Blanche Bruce, Hiram Revels, Andrew Johnson, Major General John Pope

Places to Visit Atlanta and Milledgeville (in Georgia)

Terms to Define congressional Reconstruction (military Reconstruction), carpetbaggers, scalawags, illiterate, terminated

Chapter 6
Thaddeus Stevens: Radical (pp. 28–31)

Thaddeus Stevens burned with an unrelenting resolve to win justice for blacks. He proved as uncompromising as Johnson. The clash between these two strong-willed leaders opened the door to one of the great trials in United States history—impeachment of President Andrew Johnson.

People to Meet Thaddeus Stevens, Robert E. Lee, Andrew Johnson

Place to Visit Gettysburg

Terms to Define antebellum, moderate, impeach (impeachment)

Chapter 7
Impeaching a President (pp. 32–35)

The fate of President Johnson rested upon a single vote. In an act of courage, Senator Edmund Ross of Kansas voted against impeachment—and in favor of preserving the balance of power between Congress and the presidency.

People to Meet Andrew Johnson, Edmund G. Ross, Thaddeus Stevens, James W. Grimes, D. R. Anthony, Ben Butler

■ INTRODUCING PART 1

Setting a Context in Space and Time

Using Maps Refer students to the map on page 26. Focus their attention on the map legend. What do students think the term *white supremacy* means? (The belief that whites are "supreme" or "higher" than other races) Point out that this was the belief in much of the white South prior to the Civil War. Challenge students to speculate on how southern states might re-establish this policy *after* the war. (Students can compare their speculations to what they read in Part 1.) Next, ask students to draw a two-column table in their notebooks. One column should be labeled "Events/Laws that Promoted Reconstruction." The other column should be labeled "Events/Laws that Worked Against Reconstruction." Direct them to fill out this chart throughout their study of Parts 1 and 2. When students are done, they will better understand how white supremacy returned to the South.

Understanding Chronology Tell the class that Reconstruction lasted until 1877. Part 1 covers only the first three years of the period. By studying the Chronology of Events on page 184, students can see in the period a preponderance of events related to issues of race and equality.

Setting a Context for Reading

Thinking about the Big Ideas You might want to open Part 1 by reading aloud the following selection from President Lincoln's Second Inaugural Address.

With malice toward none; with charity for all; . . . let us strive on to . . . bind up the nation's wounds; to care for him who shall have borne the battle, and for his widow, and his orphan—to do all which may achieve and cherish a just, and a lasting peace. . . .

Ask students to explain how Lincoln might describe a "just peace" for the South. Now read aloud the quote by Thaddeus Stevens on page 12 of this Guide. How do Stevens's ideas of justice for the South differ from those of Lincoln? Use this discussion to lead into the questions raised by the author on page 12 of Chapter 1: "How should the North treat its former enemy? Should it be punished?" How would Lincoln answer these questions? How would Stevens answer them? How would students answer them?

■ DISCUSSING PART 1

Understanding the Chapters

The following questions can serve as a guide to discussing each chapter. (Page references and suggested answers or tips are in parentheses.)

Chapter 1

1. The author wants to know: Did you ever lose a fight? Were you embarrassed and angry? How do these feelings help you better understand the way white Southerners felt at the end of the war? (p. 12. Answers will vary.

But lead students to understand that even when the war ended the nation was still divided emotionally and spiritually.)

2. Suppose you were a fact finder sent South by the president in 1866. What two problems would you say were most critical? Why? (pp. 12–14. Possible responses: Economic collapse, destruction of property, lack of government and order, need to help African Americans, etc. Students might point out how each of these conditions threatened reunion.)

Note: See Thinking about the Big Ideas for the author's questions on page 12. See Debating the Issues and Making Ethical Judgments for the author's questions on page 14.

Chapter 2

1. What strengths did Andrew Johnson bring to political office? (pp. 15–16. Good speaking ability, loyalty to Union, courage)

2. What weaknesses undermined his success? (p. 16. Stubbornness, unwillingness to compromise)

3. The author wants to know: What is a folly? (p. 16. A silly or foolish act) What and when was the Louisiana Purchase? (p. 16. Territory west of the Mississippi purchased from France in 1803; see Book 4.)

Chapter 3

1. What was some of the work done by the Freedmen's Bureau? (pp. 17–18. Provided food, clothing, and shelter for needy blacks and whites; educated freedmen and freedwomen)

2. How did some white Southerners deny justice to blacks? (pp. 19–20. Passed black codes, attacked blacks, formed hate groups such as the Ku Klux Klan, etc.)

3. The author wants to know: Did Southerners have the right to send former Confederate officers and officials to Congress? (p. 20. Answers will vary. Open discussion by asking whether Confederates had committed an act of treason by seceding. Why or why not?)

4. The author wants to know: What was going on in the South at the start of Reconstruction? (p. 20. To encourage discussion, have students answer this question from each of the following perspectives: a white Southerner, a white Northerner, a freedman or freedwoman, President Johnson.)

5. The author wants to know: What were the unsettled issues at the end of the war? (p. 20. Students should realize that although the questions of slavery and of a state's right to leave the union had been answered officially, in reality there were many unanswered feelings and ideas about both.)

Chapter 4

1. What were the provisions of the 13th Amendment? (p. 21. Outlawed slavery)

2. The author wants to know: If you are free and can't vote, are you really free? If some laws still restrict your movement, are you free? (p. 21. Answers will vary, but lead students to understand that justice for African Americans who had been enslaved meant winning equality before the law.)

3. What was the purpose of the Civil Rights Act of 1866? (p. 22. To nullify the black codes)

4. How did the 14th Amendment affect the balance of power between state and federal governments? (p. 23. It took power from the states and gave it to the Supreme Court.)

5. How did this amendment help protect the inalienable rights of all citizens? (p. 23. It allowed the federal government to declare unfair state laws unconstitutional. This helped ensure the constitutional principle of fairness for all.)

Note: See Making Ethical Judgments for the author's questions on page 23.

Chapter 5

1. Who were some of the Northerners who headed South? Why did each group go? (pp. 24–25. Soldiers—to guarantee black freedom; carpetbaggers—to help govern or to turn a quick profit; workers for the Freedmen's Bureau—to help ease the misery of war and to teach African Americans)

2. What were the provisions of the Reconstruction Act? (p. 25. Each southern state had to write a new Constitution true to the U.S. Constitution; all males over 21 could vote, except criminals and former Confederate officials.)

3. How did the Reconstruction Act change politics in the South and the nation as a whole? (pp. 24–26. In the South, blacks won election at the local, state, and national levels. In the North, however, there were too few black voters to overcome white prejudice toward the idea of black politicians.)

Chapter 6

1. What early problems did Thaddeus Stevens overcome? (p. 28. Poverty, an alcoholic father, a physical handicap)

2. What character traits helped make him a strong politician? (pp. 28–29. Possible responses: a good mind, fierce honesty, a good business sense, a commitment to the principle of equality for all)

3. What major difference separated Stevens and Johnson? (pp. 26–27. Stevens felt the federal government should ensure fair treatment of blacks. Johnson felt that job belonged to the states.)

4. How does the Constitution make it difficult to remove a president from office? (p. 31. After students have looked up the definitions of *treason, bribery,* and *misdemeanor,* discuss with the class what might be entailed in proving a president guilty of such.)

5. The author wants to know: Do you think Stevens will be able to impeach Johnson? (p. 31. Use this open-ended discussion to bridge Chapters 6 and 7.)

Chapter 7

1. Why did so much pressure surround Edmund Ross? (p. 32. Because he was the only senator who had not stated in advance how he would vote, and the necessary two-thirds vote for impeachment was one vote short)

2. Suppose Ross had voted for impeachment. How would his vote have affected the system of checks and balances? Why? (p. 34. It would have made Congress the most powerful branch of government, because Congress could remove leaders on the basis of personality rather than illegal conduct.)

Making Connections

Use this activity to help students link the big ideas across chapters.

Assign groups of students to draw a chart comparing Presidential Reconstruction with Congressional Reconstruction. To get students started, you might draw the following incomplete chart on the chalkboard.

	Goals	Methods of Achieving	Results
Presidential Reconstruction			
Congressional Reconstruction			

Debating the Issues

The topics below can stimulate debate. (Points to consider are in parentheses.)

1. *Resolved:* That slaves should be paid for all their years of past suffering and work. (You might conduct this debate in the form of a courtroom scene in which some students take the part of African Americans who testify about the amount and/or value of their labor while they were enslaved. Lawyers might also include some of the "legal eagles" mentioned on page 17.)

2. *Resolved:* That, aside from the Bill of Rights, the 14th Amendment is the most important of all the amendments. (The author notes this claim on book page 33.

Assign students to study other amendments prior to organizing the debate. Students debating the "con" side should select at least two other amendments they believe are more important than the 14th.)

Making Ethical Judgments

The following questions ask students to consider issues of ethics. (Points to consider are in parentheses.)

1. On page 14, the author asks: Without land, without law and order, without civil rights backed by guarantees, what did "freedom" mean? Suppose you were a freedman or freedwoman in 1865. How would you have answered this question? As the author asks on page 23, what does freedom mean to you, today? (Answers will vary widely. To help students answer this question, you might have them list the conditions endured by enslaved Africans. Which of these conditions had been ended by the war? What new restrictions on liberty had emerged? Even without full freedom, would most freedmen or freedwomen return to the past? Why or why not?)

2. Imagine you had been Edmund Ross. How would you have explained your decision to vote according to your conscience instead of according to the will of Kansas voters? (Most students will indicate the need to preserve the balance of power among the three branches of government. Ask volunteers to explain what they would have done if they had been in Ross's shoes. Would they have voted for impeachment? Why or why not?)

■ PROJECTS AND ACTIVITIES

Writing Historical Fiction Working individually or in small groups, students can write fictional accounts of a former Confederate soldier's homecoming. Stories can be written from the point of view of the soldier, his family, and those he had formerly enslaved. Writers should include a description of the physical destruction to the South and dialogues that reveal characters' feelings about the war. Allow time for students to read their stories aloud. (Some students might wish to write and enact dramatic scenes, instead.)

Designing Commemorative Stamps Remind students that February is Black History Month. Have them imagine they have been asked by the federal government to create a series of commemorative stamps on "famous firsts" achieved during Reconstruction. With the class, brainstorm a list of personal and national achievements. Then assign small groups of students to design poster-sized designs for each of the people or events named.

Analyzing a Quote In 1866, Frederick Douglass declared:

The arm of the Federal government is long, but it is far too short to protect the rights of individuals in the interior of distant States. They must have the power to protect themselves, or they will go unprotected, in spite of all the laws the Federal government can put upon the national statute-book.

Read this quote aloud. Then ask students to name examples of injustice that Douglass might have used to support his opinion. What "power" might Douglass have thought was necessary to protect blacks? (The power to elect local officials to protect them)

Writing a Dialogue Distribute copies of the above quote by Douglass. Then divide the class into groups. Direct half the groups to create dialogues in which President Johnson addresses Douglass's concerns. The other half should create dialogues in which Thaddeus Stevens speaks to Douglass. Call on volunteers to read their dialogues aloud. How do the dialogues differ? What do they reveal about the attitudes of Johnson and Stevens toward Reconstruction?

Recognizing Prejudice Read aloud or distribute copies of the following black code enacted by Mississippi.

It shall be unlawful for any officer, station agent, collector, or employee on any railroad in this State, to allow any freedman . . . to ride in any first class passenger cars . . . used by . . . white persons.

Ask students what this law says about the relationship between blacks and whites. How does it put black Southerners in a slave-like position? How does the law illustrate the concept of prejudice?

Drawing a Flowchart You can assign more advanced students to study the impeachment process by studying Article 1, Sections 2 and 3 in the Constitution. Ask them to make flowcharts to illustrate the impeachment process, and then to use the charts to explain the process to the class. Next, call on volunteers to use these flowcharts to trace impeachment proceedings against Andrew Johnson. At what stage in the process were proceedings halted? Suppose Johnson had been impeached? What would have happened next? (Interested students may wish to compare the Johnson proceedings to the Watergate proceedings against President Richard Nixon in 1974.)

Note from the Author

Back in 1892, Woodrow Wilson served as a member of a famous committee of ten charged to look at America's schools. That committee suggested a history-centered curriculum for all children, not just the college-bound, because "it best promotes that invaluable mental power that we call judgment."

■ BRIDGING THE PARTS

Analyzing a Quote Tell students that black historian and scholar W.E.B. DuBois summed up Reconstruction in the following words.

The slave went free; stood a brief moment in the sun; then moved back again toward slavery.

Call on students to state in their own words DuBois's opinion of Reconstruction. In the years between 1865 and 1876, how did African Americans "stand in the sun"? What events pushed them back toward slavery? Tell students that in Part 2 they will learn how Reconstruction came to an end.

■ STUDY GUIDE

The Study Guide appears on page 50. Guidelines and page references for answers are provided below.

1. (a) p. 12 (b) pp. 15–19, 22–23 (c) p. 17 (d) p. 20 (e) p. 25–26 (f) pp. 25–26 (g) pp. 28–31 (h) pp. 32–34

2. (a) pp. 13–14; Physical destruction, displaced people (b) p. 19; Race riots (c) p. 20; Instruction of former slaves (d) p. 27; Economic activity of a "New South"

3. (a) pp. 17–18 (b) pp. 18–19 (c) p. 24 (d) p. 24 (e) p. 24 (f) p. 30

4. pp. 13, 16; Through immigration and through the purchase of Alaska

5. (a) pp. 19–20; Terrorized blacks who sought to exercise their rights (b) p. 19; Limited the legal rights of blacks and imposed segregation (c) pp. 19–20; Exposed blacks and whites to violence and murder

6. Provisions listed on page 25. (a) Might have supported them because of new economic and political opportunities for Northerners who headed into the South (b) Probably supported them because Northerners gave scalawags a role in government (c) Probably supported them because of increased political rights (d) Probably opposed them because of restricted political role and new opportunities extended to blacks

7. pp. 30–31; Answers will vary, but most arguments will focus on Johnson's support of states' rights, his willingness to allow former Confederate officers and officials to resume power, and his unwillingness to use federal power to guarantee liberty and justice to black Southerners.

8. pp. 31–35; Answers will vary.

9. Obituaries will vary, but most blacks regarded Stevens as a hero and a champion of liberty.

10. The 14th Amendment guaranteed that no state could unjustly infringe upon liberties guaranteed by the Constitution. It limited states' rights by giving the Supreme Court the power to declare state laws unconstitutional. This amendment would give the Court the tool to overturn laws and court decisions that denied citizens "due process of law."

Note from the Author

I've written a storyteller's history. It is intellectual history. It starts with the belief that children can handle complex ideas and that they enjoy being challenged. It is a history that celebrates our free, democratic form of government. Some critics may find it jingoistic. I don't think it is. I don't neglect the horrors and mistakes of our past. But there is a big difference in forms of government, and I believe we are fortunate in our heritage. I tell my readers that. I also tell them that this is my opinion and they are free to challenge it. I'm told that the books provoke much discussion. That is my intention.

PART 2
Retreat from the South (Chapters 8–10)

The Big Ideas

In 1875, near the end of Reconstruction, Ralph Waldo Emerson wrote:

We hoped that in the peace . . . a great expansion would follow in the mind of the country, grand views in every direction. . . . But the energy of the nation seems to have expended itself.

The passions of civil war and the fury of Radical Reconstruction had left the nation exhausted. The 13th, 14th, and 15th Amendments remained enduring accomplishments. But federal enforcement of these amendments lay nearly a century ahead. In the late 1870s, the nation abandoned black Southerners to chart their own fates. Part 2 describes the twilight of Reconstruction and the retreat of Northern troops from the South.

Chapter Summaries

Each of the three chapters in Part 2 describes the collapse of Reconstruction. The stories are as follows.

Chapter 8

Welcome to Meeting Street (pp. 36–39)

Reconstruction legislatures prompted some people to talk of "America's Second Revolution." But this revolution lacked the full commitment of a broad-based citizenry. Slowly, but surely, former Confederate officers and officials organized "Redeemer" governments that pushed blacks out of politics.

People to Meet Robert Brown Elliott, Eric Foner, Francis Louis Cardozo, Thaddeus Stevens, Robert Smalls, William Beverly Nash, Franklin J. Moses, Jr., Daniel Henry Chamberlain, Thomas J. Robertson, Jonathan C. Gibbs, Adies Ball

Places to Visit Charleston (in South Carolina), Beaufort (in North Carolina), Columbia (in South Carolina)

Terms to Define ubiquitous, "Redeemer" governments

Chapter 9

A Southern Girl's Diary (pp. 40–43)

African Americans who had been enslaved, such as the Montgomery family, briefly tasted the joy of land ownership and free enterprise. Their success made the reconfiscation of lands by former Confederate officers and officials even more bitter—and more unjust.

People to Meet Mary Virginia Montgomery, Jefferson Davis, Andrew Johnson, Thaddeus Stevens, Benjamin Montgomery, Joseph Davis, William Montgomery, Isaiah Montgomery, General Ulysses S. Grant, Mary Lewis Montgomery, Rebecca Montgomery

Places to Visit Fort Monroe (in Virginia), Vicksburg (in Mississippi), Mound Bayou and Davis Bend (in Mississippi), Frankfort (in Kentucky)

Chapter 10

A Failed Revolution (pp. 44–48)

Corruption, lack of leadership, and lack of popular support for Reconstruction allowed the old guard to slip back into power in the South. In 1877, a political deal led President Rutherford Hayes to call an end to Reconstruction. By the end of the decade, black Southerners found themselves under the lash of a new master—a fool named Jim Crow.

People to Meet Ulysses S. Grant, Rutherford B. Hayes, Eric Foner, Robert Brown Elliott, Edward L. Ayers, Wade Hampton, D. H.

Chamberlain, F. L. Cardozo, Benjamin Tillman

Terms to Define sharecropping, poll tax, poll, lynching, segregation, Jim Crow, redeemers (Redeemer Democrats)

■ INTRODUCING PART 2

Setting a Context in Space and Time

Linking Geography to Politics Refer students back to the map on page 26. Tell them to substitute the words "Democratic power" for "white supremacy" in the map legend. With this change in mind, what can they infer about the shift in political power in the South by 1877? (That it had shifted to the Democrats) Next, challenge students to speculate on reasons white Southerners might support the Democratic party. (Lead students to recognize the link between the Republicans and Reconstruction.) Tell students that Part 2 traces the retreat of the Republicans out of the South.

Understanding Chronology Reconstruction forms a distinct era in United States history. Ask students to recall its span (1865–1877). Have students skim the Chronology on page 184 of the book to find events relating to issues of race and equality that followed 1877. What items prove that Radical Reconstruction was, as the author suggests, "a failed revolution"? (Both the 1883 *Plessy v. Ferguson* decision and the 1892 exposé of lynching)

Setting a Context for Reading

Thinking about the Big Ideas You might begin discussion by writing the title of Part 2 on the chalkboard: "Retreat from the South." Ask students what the term *retreat* means to them. (Going backward or withdrawing) Who do they think would be most likely to retreat from this region? (Federal troops, carpetbaggers, Radical Republicans, etc.) If these groups did withdraw, what do students think might happen to the struggle for equal justice

for blacks? Why? What changes would this bring about for blacks and whites in the South?

■ DISCUSSING PART 2

Understanding the Chapters

The following questions can serve as a guide to discussing each chapter. (Page references, and suggested answers or tips are in parentheses.)

Chapter 8

1. What was remarkable about the 1868 South Carolina constitutional convention? (pp. 36–38. The number of talented black representatives)

2. What were some of the difficult questions faced by Reconstruction legislatures? (p. 39. Questions revolving around distribution of land, treatment of former Confederate officers and officials, extension of justice, creation of an interracial society, etc.)

3. What did these legislatures achieve? (p. 39. Voted for free public schools, built roads, treated former Confederates fairly)

4. How did the "Redeemer" governments seize power? (p. 39. By using fear to keep blacks from the polls)

Chapter 9

1. How did the Montgomery family gain control of Davis Bend? (p. 42. First rented the land, then raised the money to buy it)

2. What freedoms did African Americans enjoy at Davis Bend? (p. 42. The right to own property and to share in the profits of their labor; the right to elect judges, sheriffs, and political leaders)

3. How did the Montgomery family lose Davis Bend? (p. 43. Power shifts allowed Jefferson Davis to reconfiscate the land.)

Chapter 10

1. What problems did Reconstruction cause in the minds of many white Southerners?

(pp. 44–45. Forced landowners to pay for improvements voted in by black lawmakers; raised the idea that perhaps their loved ones had died for a mistaken notion about slavery)

2. The author wants to know: What did author Eric Foner mean [in the quotation in the margin on page 45]? (p. 45. That when Reconstruction ended, the federal government withdrew from the struggle for equal rights) Was the idea reborn? When? (Ask students to share what they know about the history of the civil rights struggle; discuss this struggle's ties to Reconstruction.)

3. How did white Southerners move to restrict the rights of blacks? (pp. 45–48. Through poll taxes, lynching, a policy of segregation, etc.)

4. How did Republicans and Redeemer Democrats differ in their view of the role of government? (p. 48. Democrats did not approve of an active government that tried to improve conditions for all people.)

Making Connections

Use the questions below to help students link the big ideas across chapters. (Suggested responses are in parentheses.)
1. What was the connection between the large black populations in the South and the interracial Reconstruction governments? (With the vote, blacks had the power to elect black officials.)
2. What was the connection between political corruption and the end of Reconstruction? (Possible response: Corruption became so widespread that it distracted Northerners from the struggle for civil rights in the South.)
3. What was the connection between white supremacy and slow economic recovery in the South? (Possible response: It stifled creativity, limited the workforce, and discouraged immigrants and big industries from heading into the region.)

Debating the Issues

The topic below can stimulate debate. (Points to consider appear in parentheses.)
Resolved: That the Confederacy lost the Civil War but won the battle against Reconstruction. (Appoint some students to defend the legal precedents set in place during Reconstruction, particularly the 13th, 14th, and 15th Amendments. Have others point out ways in which white supremacists undermined the principles of justice for all and "due process of law."

Making Ethical Judgments

The following activity asks students to consider issues of ethics. (Points to consider are in parentheses.) Thaddeus Stevens volunteered to defend Jefferson Davis.

Why do you think Stevens took this position? Do you agree? (Lead students to understand that Stevens believed in universal justice. You might ask some of your more able students to review John Adams's defense of soldiers involved in the Boston Massacre. How were the ethical decisions faced by Adams and Stevens similar?)

■ PROJECTS AND ACTIVITIES

Writing a News Story Working individually or in groups, students can imagine they are reporters for a northern newspaper. Their task is to cover the South Carolina constitutional convention. Tell students to be sure to answer the six reporter questions: *Who? What? When? Where? Why? How?* To get students started, you might distribute copies of the following incomplete article.

Integration comes to South Carolina
by (student's name)
Charleston, SC, January 14, 1868. The black delegates who walked into the fashionable Charleston Clubhouse wrote history today.

Using Historical Imagination Jefferson Davis never stood trial. But suppose he had? Ask students to design a skit in which they speculate on how the trial might have progressed. Tell students to select one of the African American "legal eagles" mentioned in Chapter 3 as prosecutor. Suggest that Thaddeus Stevens serve as the defense attorney. Other students should take the parts of the interracial jury pictured on page 40. Still other students should act as witnesses. At the end of the skit, allow time for members of the jury to present their verdict. Is Davis guilty or not guilty of high treason against the United States?

Designing a Historical Marker Direct students to prepare historical markers for the sites of the black communities at Davis Bend and Mound Bayou. What reasons would students cite for preserving these places as national landmarks?

Drawing Political Cartoons Refer students to the political cartoons in Chapter 10. Then have them work in small groups to design political cartoons expressing their opinions of Reconstruction.

■ BRIDGING THE PARTS

Stating the Problem Read aloud a description of the mood among freedpeople written by a black Texan in 1879.

> *There are no words which can fully express . . . the real condition of my people throughout the south, nor how deeply and keenly they feel the necessity of fleeing from the . . . long pent-up hatred of their old masters which they feel assured will . . . burst loose like the pent-up fires of a volcano and crush them if they remain here many years longer.*

What problem did the writer foresee for black Southerners at the end of Reconstruction? (Pent-up anger of former slave owners) What action does the speaker feel they must take? (Flee the region) Tell students that in the late 1870s many blacks saw a new escape route—flight onto the unsettled Plains. Expansion into this last region claimed by Native Americans forms the subject of Part 3.

■ STUDY GUIDE

The Study Guide appears on page 51. Guidelines and page references for answers are provided below.

1. (a) pp. 36–37, 39 (b) p. 38 (c) pp. 40–42 (d) pp. 40–41, 43 (e) p. 45 (f) p. 47 (g) pp. 45–46

2. (a) p. 36 (b) p. 41 (c) pp. 41–42 (d) p. 42

3. (a) p. 44 (b) p. 45 (c) p. 46 (d) p. 46 (e) p. 48

4. pp. 36–38; The interracial composition of the meeting

5. p. 42; Advertisements might highlight the right to enjoy the profits of one's own labor. They might also mention the right of African American members of the community to elect their own officials.

6. p. 43; Answers will vary, but students will probably note that the Montgomery family legally bought the land. The fact that Davis won his claim reveals the disregard for black rights in courts of law.

7. p. 45; For his inability to enforce Reconstruction or to curb corruption within his own government

8. pp. 45–46; By abolishing slavery the 13th Amendment gave all constitutional rights to African Americans. (a) The 15th Amendment guaranteed universal manhood suffrage to blacks. Poll taxes restricted that right. (a–c) The 14th Amendment guaranteed "due process of law" and "equal protection of the laws." The intent of both poll taxes and segregated railroad cars refused blacks these rights. Lynchings clearly violated the "due process" clause, by exacting execution (murder) without benefit of a trial and jury.

9. p. 48; Dr. Martin Luther King, Jr. (Encourage students to do further research on Dr. King's role in a second Reconstruction.)

10. Reconstruction legislatures allowed black voters and politicians to take part in the political process. They levied taxes according to income so that governments could finance public education, roads, and other public improvements meant to benefit all people. All of these changes are part of our government today.

PART 3
Battle for the West (Chapters 11–18)

The Big Ideas

Native Americans saw the sprawling Great Plains differently than did the settlers who would one day take the land from them. Explained Chief Luther Standing Bear of the Oglala Sioux:

We did not think of the great open plains . . . . as "wild." Only to the white man was nature a "wilderness." . . . To us it was tame. . . . Not until [settlers] from the east came and with brutal frenzy heaped injustices upon us . . . was it "wild" for us.

In the late 1800s, the trail of broken treaties that had robbed Native American peoples of their lands finally headed onto the Great Plains. Here Native Americans waged their last battles. Part 3 describes the changes that settlement of the Plains brought to Native Americans—and to the nation as a whole.

Chapter Summaries

The eight chapters in Part 3 trace the nation's march across the last continental frontier. The stories are as follows.

Chapter 11

Meanwhile, Out West (pp. 49–51)

No sooner had the Civil War ended than settlers spilled onto the Great Plains. Here settlers battled Native Americans and the environment to turn the prairies into the nation's "breadbasket."

People to Meet John Wesley Powell, Walt Whitman

Places to Visit Wisconsin Cutover, Colorado River, Grand Canyon, Guthrie (in Oklahoma Territory), Chicago, Lincoln (in Nebraska)

Term to Define capital

Chapter 12

Riding the Trail (pp. 52–57)

For a brief period, much of the Great Plains belonged to the Texas longhorns and cattle-herders who rode the open range. The meeting of cattle trails and railroad lines created "cowtowns" still famous in western lore—Abilene, Dodge City, Wichita, and more.

People to Meet Elijah McCoy, Bill McCoy, Joseph G. McCoy, Jesse Chisholm, Nat Love (Deadwood Dick), Eddie Foy, Elizabeth E. Johnson, James Butler "Wild Bill" Hickok, Bat Masterson, Wyatt Earp, Tom Mix, Martha Jane Cannary (Calamity Jane)

Places to Visit Abilene (in Kansas), Chicago, Texas panhandle, Red River, Tombstone (in Arizona), Dodge City (in Kansas, Chisholm Trail, Wichita (in Kansas), Dakota Territory, Fort Laramie

Terms to Define range, Texas longhorns

Chapter 13

Rails Across the Country (pp. 58–63)

On May 10, 1869, crews for the Central Pacific and the Union Pacific met at Promontory Point in Utah. The coming together of the two railroad lines marked the completion of the nation's first transcontinental railroad. Bands of iron now drew East and West together, adding new meaning to the term *United* States.

People to Meet Leland Stanford, Thomas Durant, Grenville Dodge, Samuel Montague, Maxine Hong Kingston, Ulysses S. Grant, Bret Harte

Places to Visit Promontory Point (in Utah), Sacramento (in California), Sierra Nevada mountains, Omaha (in Nebraska), Green River, Citadel Rock, Wasatch range, Great Salt Lake

Terms to Define ties, visionaries, subsidy, graders, tracklayers, gaugers, spikers, bolters, meridian

Chapter 14

Taking the Train (pp. 64–67)

For passengers, traveling the transcontinental railroad was one of the great experiences of the late 1800s. The travelers got to see firsthand the landscape that had thrilled their imaginations. But for Native Americans, the "iron horses" spelled disaster and the end of a way of life.

People to Meet Meriwether Lewis, Walt Whitman, William L. Humason, George Pullman, James Boys (Frank and Jesse)

Places to Visit Weber Canyon, Platte River, Missouri River, Council Bluffs, Omaha (in Nebraska), Cheyenne (in Wyoming), Salt Lake City (in Utah), Deseret (in Utah)

Terms to Define vicariously, Thousand-Mile Tree, "Big Muddy," emigrant cars, iron horse, paternalistic, welfare capitalism

Chapter 15

Fencing the Homestead (pp. 68–75)

Once settlers moved into the "Great American Desert," they used technology—windmills, barbed wire, and iron plows—to transform the environment into a sprawling agricultural region.

People to Meet William Inge, Stephen Vincent Benét, Brewster Higley, Oliver Hudson Kelley, Joseph Glidden, Willa Cather, William Cullen Bryant

Places to Visit Plains states, Far West, Yellowstone National Park, Great Plains

Terms to Define forty-niners, Great American Desert, Homestead Act, bison, pronghorns, the Grange, grangers, husbandry, barbed

wire, savannas, prairie, steppe, domestic animals

Chapter 16

Reaping a Harvest (pp. 76–79)

The McCormick reaper did to wheat farming what Eli Whitney's cotton gin did to cotton growing. It made big farms practical—and profitable.

People to Meet Cyrus McCormick, John Deere, Everett Dick, Mark Alfred Carleton, Luther Burbank, George Washington Carver

Places to Visit Shenandoah Valley, Chicago, Minneapolis, London, Santa Rosa (in California), Tuskegee (in Alabama)

Terms to Define sod, dour, reaper, scythe, King Wheat, installment buying, Morrill Act, Hatch Act

Chapter 17

The Trail Ends on a Reservation (pp. 80–88)

Native Americans and settlers had incompatible lives. Neither wanted to accommodate the other. In an uneven power struggle, Native Americans found themselves pushed onto unwanted lands called reservations. With the 1890 battle at Wounded Knee, the last western frontier closed.

People to Meet Crazy Horse, Buffalo Bill Cody, Chief Kicking Bird, George Armstrong Custer, Philip Sheridan, William Tecumseh Sherman, John Pope, John M. Chivington, Many Lightnings, Ohiyesa (Charles Eastman), Seth Eastman, Sitting Bull, Henry Benjamin Whipple

Places to Visit Little Big Horn River; Carlisle (in Pennsylvania), Pine Ridge Agency School (in Dakota), Wounded Knee

Terms to Define compatible, iron horses, reservations, paupers, "final solution," Nazis, Buffalo Soldiers

Chapter 18

The People of the Pierced Noses (pp. 89–94)

In one last bid for freedom, Chief Joseph led the Nez Perce on a desperate flight into

Canada. His plea in behalf of the Nez Perce confined to reservations has become an eloquent statement of justice for people of all races and backgrounds.

People to Meet Chief Joseph (Hin-mah-too-yah-laht-ket), Crazy Horse, Sitting Bull, Black Hawk, Geronimo, Stephen Vincent Benét, George Armstrong Custer, Meriwether Lewis, William Clark, Thomas Jefferson, Ollokot, Ulysses S. Grant, Alvin M. Josephy, Jr., Looking Glass, Emma and George Cowan, Chester Fee, General Howard

Places to Visit Wounded Knee, Bear Paw Mountain, Yellowstone National Park

■ INTRODUCING PART 3

Setting a Context in Space and Time

Using Maps To set the stage for the environmental changes that settlement brought to the Great Plains, refer students to the map on page 75. Ask what land forms bounded the Great Plains on the east and west. (Mississippi River and Rocky Mountains) What nations set its northern and southern limits? (Canada and Mexico)

Next, ask students to identify some of the forms of wildlife shown on the map. Then request a volunteer to look up the term *prairie* in a class dictionary. What does it mean? (Meadow or area of rolling grasslands) Why would this environment support such a wide variety of wildlife? (Provided a huge grazing area) Challenge students to speculate on what changes settlers would bring to this environment. Save the speculations for review as students work their way through Part 3.

Interpreting a Time Table To provide an overview of the effect of settlement on Native Americans, have students turn to the time table on page 88. What has happened to Native Americans since the arrival of the first European settlers? (Their independence has

been steadily diminished.) What items in the time table show the restriction of Native American rights during the 1800s? When did Native Americans finally become United States citizens? Remind students of the title of the first book in *A History of US: The First Americans.* What irony (twist of fate) does this time table point out about Native Americans? (Although Native American were the first to settle what is now the United States, they were the last group to receive citizenship.)

Setting a Context for Reading

Thinking about the Big Ideas You might open discussion by having students read the titles of the eight chapters in Part 3. Then have students predict changes that came to the West in the years following the Civil War. Refer students first to the poster on page 49 and then to the map on page 55. What changes can they infer from these sources? (The settlement of prairie land where Native Americans lived)

Next, encourage students to put themselves in the shoes of Native Americans at the time. How would they feel at the sight of cattle trails, railroads, and homesteaders crossing their land? (Anger, a sense of loss) How would settlers feel about the same sights? (Pride, a sense of growth) You may want to read aloud the quote by Chief Luther Standing Bear on page 23 of this Guide. How did Native Americans and settlers view the plains? How might these different views lead to "injustices" for Native Americans?

■ DISCUSSING PART 3

Understanding the Chapters

The following questions can serve as a guide to discussing each chapter. (Page references and suggested answers or tips are in parentheses.)

Chapter 11

1. What was the war in the West about? (p. 49. Control of the land)

2. What led settlers to move onto Native American lands? (pp. 49–50. Many held mistaken ideas about Native Americans and rights to the land. An economic depression and lack of land in the East also pushed people onto the Plains.)

3. The author wants to know: How could Chicago grow into an important port? (p. 51. As a tip, refer students to the map on page 55. Ask them to locate Chicago on the Great Lakes. Also note all the railroad links to major rivers.)

4. What types of growth does Whitman mention in his poem? (p. 51. Growth of cities, growth of commerce, growth of communication, growth of transportation, etc.)

Chapter 12

1. What developments helped turn cattle raising into a profitable business? (pp. 52–53. The westward expansion of the railroads; opening of cattle trails to shipping centers such as Abilene; development of refrigerated railroad cars; demand for beef)

2. What hardships did cowboys face along the trail? (pp. 53–54. Bad weather, attacks by Native Americans and rustlers, thirst, stampedes, etc.)

3. Why was there greater democracy on the cattle trails than in other areas of American life? (p. 56. Because people were judged by their ability, not the color of their skin, accent in their speech, or sex)

4. What parts of a cowhand's life were influenced by the region's Spanish heritage? (p. 56. Clothing styles, lingo)

5. The author wants to know: What does the nickname "Calamity Jane" tell you about Martha Jane Cannary? (p. 57. That a lot of trouble came her way)

Chapter 13

1. What hardships and obstacles did the Central Pacific and Union Pacific have to overcome? (pp. 59–60. Had to carry all their supplies with them; had to cut paths through many natural barriers; had to find workers willing to do the hard labor)

2. What role did immigrants and African Americans play in building the first transcontinental railroad? (p. 60. Largely Chinese crews laid track for the Central Pacific, while Irish immigrants and African Americans worked for the Union Pacific.)

3. What legal and illegal methods did railroad owners use to finance construction? (pp. 59–63. *Legal:* government subsidies, sale of stocks, low wages. *Illegal:* crooked contracts, overcharging the government, unsafe workmanship)

4. What were the long-term effects of the transcontinental railroad? (p. 63. Tied the nation together; speeded transportation of people and goods; made the country seem smaller)

Chapter 14

1. The author wants to know: Where is the Platte? (p. 64. Students can locate the Platte River on the map on page 55.)

2. How was the transcontinental railroad like the Northwest Passage sought by Europeans? (p. 64. It connected the "Eastern and Western seas," or the Atlantic and Pacific oceans.)

3. How did the emigrant cars and the Pullman cars differ from each other? (pp. 65–66. Emigrant cars were low-priced, modest coaches. Pullman cars offered far greater comfort and luxury including beds and meals.)

4. The author wants to know: What is meant by the term *welfare capitalism?* (p. 67. System in which the factory owner provides for—and hence determines—the welfare or well-being of workers)

Chapter 15

1. Why did farmers have a hard time growing crops on the Plains? (pp. 68–69. Stampeding cattle, few trees, little water, extremes in weather, invasions of grasshoppers, etc.)

2. Despite problems, why did so many people head onto the Plains? (p. 69. Scarce land in the East; low prices for public lands in the West)

3. How did homesteaders solve some of the problems of farming on the Plains? (pp. 68–72. Built windmills for water, used barbed wire to fence in gardens)

4. What conditions helped end cattle drives? (pp. 72–73. Fenced-in land, growth of railroads)

5. How did farming change in the late 1800s? (p. 73. Became a big business)

Chapter 16

1. How did John Deere's plow revolutionize agriculture? (p. 76. Provided a way to cut through the tough prairie soil)

2. How did Cyrus McCormick's reaper bring even greater changes to agriculture? (pp. 76–77. By speeding up harvest time, it made big farms practical and profitable.)

3. How did McCormick help expand the Industrial Revolution? (p. 77. He set up factories in the rural Midwest. With the installment plan, he increased demand for reapers and speeded the mechanization of agriculture.)

4. What were some of the negative effects of the farming revolution? (pp. 78–79. Small farmers found it difficult to compete; farmers became less self-sufficient and more dependent upon market demand; poor farming methods opened the land to erosion.)

5. What actions were taken against these negative effects? (p. 79. Congress passed the Morill and Hatch acts; scientists researched new developments in agriculture.)

Chapter 17

1. Why couldn't Native Americans and homesteaders exist on the same land? (p. 80. Plains Indians were mostly hunters, while the homesteaders were farmers or ranchers. Hunters roamed the open land; farmers and ranchers cleared the land and fenced it in.)

2. The author wants to know: When did Lewis and Clark explore the West? (p. 80. See Book 4. 1804–1806.)

3. In what way did Native Americans and other Americans organize society differently? (pp. 81–82. Native American societies usually centered on the community, rather than on the individual. Other Americans emphasized individualism.)

4. Why were Native Americans sent to reservations? (p. 82. To move them off land that other Americans wanted)

5. What attitude did Philip Sheridan, John Pope, and William Tecumseh Sherman take toward the Native Americans? (pp. 82–83. That they should be wiped out.)

Note: See Debating the Issues for the author's question on page 82. See Making Ethical Judgments for the author's questions on pages 85 and 88.

Chapter 18

1. In what order did newcomers arrive on Nez Perce land? (pp. 90–91. Explorers [Lewis and Clark]; trappers and traders; gold miners; ministers and homesteaders)

2. The author wants to know: How long after the visit of Lewis and Clark did the first United States commissioners meet with Chief Joseph? (p. 91. Seventy-one years)

3. Why did the flight of Chief Joseph capture so much attention? (p. 92. Although outnumbered and outgunned, the Nez Perce—including many women, children, and old people—managed to escape and outwit federal troops.)

4. What rights did Chief Joseph demand for the Nez Perce? (p. 94. To move about freely; to be subject to the same laws and government as the whites)

Making Connections

Use these questions to help students link the big ideas across the chapters. (Suggested responses are in parentheses.)

1. How did the growth of the railroad help end the way of life for Native Americans on the Plains? (Led to the sale of Native American land, destruction of the buffalo, and the flood of homesteaders onto the Plains.)

2. How did the spread of the Industrial Revolution onto the Plains change farming in the United States? (The use of farm machinery required capital, which in turn helped make farming into a big business.)

Debating the Issues

Use the topic below to stimulate debate. (Points to consider are in parentheses.)

Resolved: That Native Americans should fight for control of their land regardless of the consequences. (On page 82 the author asks students if they would be willing to leave their homes for a reservation. Ask some students to act as U. S. commissioners sent to talk Native Americans into resettling on reservations. Others should imagine they are members of a Native American council who must debate the proposals.)

Making Ethical Judgments

The following questions ask students to consider issues of ethics. (Points to consider are in parentheses.)

1. On page 85, the author explores what happens when one group of people have a home and another group either wants that home or has no home at all. Is there any way people can share their resources so that everybody has a place to live? (These are tough questions. First, consider the Native Americans. Land in the East was becoming scarce. Does that mean that the government was justified in taking Native American land on the Plains? Then, what about the homeless today? Does society, or the community, have a responsibility to care for them? Why or why not?

2. On page 88 the author asks whether other Americans might have cooperated with Native Americans rather than trying to conquer them. Would it have worked? (There are no easy ways for us today to comprehend the feelings about Native Americans that prevailed in the nineteenth century. However, students should keep those feelings in mind when they discuss these issues.)

3. On page 88 the author also asks whether you think modern industrial cultures have a duty to protect native peoples and their natural environments. Or should the native cultures be forced to learn new ways of life? (Review the changes forced upon Native Americans. Next, focus on a native culture resisting changes today—Native Americans in the Amazon rain forests, Masai on the savannas of East Africa, the nomads of Tibet. Are modern cultures helping or hurting by trying to teach these people new ways of living?)

■ PROJECTS AND ACTIVITIES

Writing a Ballad Tell students that cowhands kept cattle from stampeding by singing ballads. Challenge students to write a "cattle lullaby" that captures life on the trail. If possible, have students locate some ballads to play in class.

Using Historical Imagination Divide the class into four groups. Have each group devise a story that one of the following might tell a grandchild about the first transcontinental railroad: (a) a Chinese railroad worker, (b) an Irish railroad worker, (c) a Cheyenne who saw the first "iron horse," (d) an Easterner who took one of the first cross-continental trips aboard an "emigrant car."

Writing Poetry Review the Stephen Vincent Benét poem on page 70. Then challenge students to write their own poems about homesteading on the Plains. Tell students to use at least three of the following words in their poems: sod, buffalo grass, grasshoppers, blizzard, drought, buffalo, prairie dog, tornado, prairie, brush fire, pioneer.

Designing an Advertisement Have students draw poster-sized advertisements for the McCormick reaper. Ads should describe advantages of the reaper and methods of payment. (Remind students that the installment plan was just as new as the reaper.)

Interpreting a Map Refer students to the map on page 83 and help them understand that all of the ceded land shown was occupied by Native Americans before the 1860s. Have them compare that amount of Native American land with the amount occupied by Native Americans in 1890. Challenge students to estimate the percentage of land lost. Have students refer to the text to find reasons for this great change in landholdings.

Doing Library Research Ask volunteers to take the author's suggestion on page 89. Have them research the lives of Crazy Horse, Sitting Bull, Black Hawk, and Geronimo, as well as other leading Native Americans such as Red Cloud. You might have students present their findings in the form of autobiographical monologues for the class.

■ BRIDGING THE PARTS

Analyzing Primary Sources Tell students that in 1890 the Superintendent of the U.S. Census made this announcement:

> *Up to and including 1880, the country had a frontier of settlement, but at present the unsettled area has been so broken into . . . that there can hardly be said to be a frontier line. . . . [W]estward movement . . . cannot, therefore, any longer have a place in the census reports.*

What change did the Superintendent declare? (End of the frontier) Do students think this means that there were no more new frontiers for Americans to cross? (Lead students to understand that *frontier* can mean any ground-breaking endeavor.) Explain that Part 4 gives students their first look at a chronological frontier—the closing years of the nineteenth century. Ask students how they feel about standing on the end of a century!

■ STUDY GUIDE

The Study Guide appears on page 52. Guidelines and page references for answers are provided below.

1. (a) p. 49 (b) p. 52 (c) pp. 52–53 (d) pp. 52–53 (e) p. 53 (f) p. 56 (g) pp. 58, 61–63 (h) pp. 66–67 (i) p. 73 (j) pp. 76–78 (k) p. 79 (l) pp. 80, 85, 90 (m) pp. 89–94

2. (a) p. 49–50; Final land rush onto Native American lands (b) p. 58; Meeting of trains that would carry buffalo hunters and settlers west (c) p. 82; Site of victory over Custer (d) p. 85; Reservation school that taught Native Americans white ways (e) p. 88; Last major resistance by Native Americans, ended in a massacre

3. (a) p. 50 (b) p. 52 (c) p. 59 (d) p. 59 (e) p. 65 (f) p. 69 (g) pp. 72–73 (h) p. 74 (i) p. 79 (j) p. 82

4. pp. 49–50, 80, 89; Native Americans saw the land as their ancestral homeland and territory granted to them by treaty. They saw it as free, open land suitable for hunting. Homesteaders disregarded Native American land rights. They saw the Plains as "wild" land to be "tamed" for farming.

5. pp. 53–57; Hardships should include points mentioned on p. 53. Benefits might include freedom and independence.

6. pp. 58–60; Telegrams should cite reasons for the event's importance.

7. pp. 72–73; Answers will vary.

8. pp. 74, 76–79; Students should cite the fertility of the land, low cost of land, and the open, flat spaces that made it possible to use large machinery such as the reaper.

9. p. 94; Definitions might mention the application of the same liberties, laws, and government to all people.

10. Answers will vary, but students should mention the injustices and loss of a way of life suffered by Native Americans. They should also note the extraordinary growth that the United States experienced as a result of settlement. Examples include expansion of transportation and the rise of commercial farming.

PART 4
Schemers and Dreamers (Chapters 19–21)

The Big Ideas

In the late 1800s, many of the nation's large cities belonged to political bosses. Bosses held onto power because they made it their business to know people's needs and to tend to the problems of everyday life. Explained Martin Lomasney, boss of Boston's South End:

> There's got to be in every ward somebody that any bloke can come to—no matter what he's done—and get help. Help, you understand, none of your law and justice, but help.

The corruption and hucksterism of the era led authors Mark Twain and Charles Dudley Warner to call the times the Gilded Age. Part 4 traces changes at the end of the Civil War that gave rise to the schemers and the dreamers of the last three decades of the century. It also looks at efforts to promote reform by exposing the injustices of political corruption.

Chapter Summaries

The three chapters in Part 4 provide a glimpse at life at the end of Reconstruction. Stories are as follows.

Chapter 19

A Villain, a Dreamer, a Cartoonist (pp. 95–100)

Bosses such as William Marcy Tweed built political machines that lay outside the system of checks and balances set up by the Constitution. Nonetheless, they found themselves checked by yet another nongovernmental power—the scathing pen of political cartoonist Thomas Nast.

People to Meet Thomas Nast, William Marcy "Boss" Tweed, Alfred Ely Beach, William Mooney, John T. Hoffman, George Washington Plunkitt, William Riordan, Thomas Edison

Place to Visit New York City

Terms to Define alderman, Tammany Hall, graft, scoundrel, patents, political machines, subway, hydraulic, pneumatic, constituents, fraud

Chapter 20

Phineas Taylor Barnum (pp. 101–104)

"There's a sucker born ever minute," declared P.T. Barnum. But Americans so enjoyed Barnum's form of hucksterism that he turned it into "The Greatest Show on Earth," the Barnum and Bailey Circus.

People to Meet Phineas T. Barnum, Chang and Eng, Charles Stratton (General Tom Thumb), Stephen Vincent Benét, Hamlin Garland, George Leybourne

Place to Visit New York City

Terms to Define humbug, egress, robber barons, reformers, circus, jumbo/*jamba*, prohibition

Chapter 21

Huck, Tom, and Friends (pp. 105–110)

Mark Twain used his pen to describe everyday life in the closing years of the century. In vivid prose, he captured the dreams, schemes, and hopes of a people.

People to Meet Samuel Langhorne Clemens (Mark Twain); Olivia, Clara, Jean, and Susy Clemens; Andrew Smith Hallidie; Bret Harte;

Ernest Hemingway; Charles Dudley Warner; Philo Remington

Places to Visit Hannibal (in Missouri), San Francisco, Hartford (in Connecticut), Crede (in Colorado)

Terms to Define mark, twain, cable cars, gripman, Gilded Age, exigencies, sumptuous

■ INTRODUCING PART 4

Setting a Context in Space and Time

Connecting Demographics and Geography In the late 1800s, the landscape of America began to change as the urban population started to grow by leaps and bounds. To illustrate this change, copy the following statistics on the chalkboard:
Rural Population: 1870—28,625,000; 1880—36,026,000; 1890—40,841,000; 1900—45,835,000
Urban Population: 1870—9,902,000; 1880—14,130,000; 1890—22,106,000; 1900—30,160,000

Have students organize these figures on a bar or line graph. Then ask: Which label best describes the United States at the end of Reconstruction—urban or rural? (Rural) Which part of the population grew the fastest in the closing decades of the 1800s? (Urban) Challenge students to speculate on some of the problems that rapid urban growth might cause. Use this activity to lead into Chapter 19.

Defining Chronological Terms You might begin Part 4 by asking students to define the term *age*. Some students might mention chronological age; others might talk about a specific stage of life, such as old age. Next, tell students that the term *age* also refers to a historical period that is characterized or strongly influenced by some feature or person. Challenge students to brainstorm some of the historical ages with which they might be familiar. (Examples include: Ice Age, Elizabethan Age, Space Age, Jazz Age) Then

tell students that Part 4 takes a look at another historic age—the Gilded Age. Ask them to imagine what that name implies.

Setting a Context for Reading

Thinking about the Big Ideas You might open Part 4 by asking students the question raised by the author on page 95: Do you ever worry about air pollution or dishonest politicians? Then tell students that these issues also concerned people in the late 1800s. As students read through Part 4, have them write down reasons pollution and corruption were problems at this time. To connect past with present, students should note changes that have eliminated or lessened these problems.

■ DISCUSSING PART 4

Understanding the Chapters

The following questions can serve as a guide to discussing each chapter. (Page references and suggested answers or tips are in parentheses.)

Chapter 19

1. Why was pollution a problem in large cities such as New York? (pp. 95–96. Possible responses: crowded living conditions, large number of horses, use of coal for fuel, lack of controls on oil refineries, limited sanitary services, etc.)

2. How did Boss Tweed build a political machine? (pp. 96–97. Took control of jobs and services, bribed officials, offered immigrants help in exchange for votes)

3. How did Alfred Ely Beach and Thomas Nast challenge Tweed's power? (pp. 97–100. *Ely:* built a subway under Tweed's nose; *Nast:* exposed Tweed in political cartoons)

Note: See Thinking about the Big Ideas for the author's question on page 95. See Projects and Activities for the author's question on page 97.

Chapter 20

1. What did P.T. Barnum mean when he called himself the Prince of Humbug? (p. 101. That he excelled at fooling people)

2. Why didn't people seem to mind being tricked by Barnum? (pp. 101–102. Because he made them laugh)

3. How did P.T. Barnum fit the age in which he lived? (p. 104. He combined extremes—a desire for money with a desire to do good.)

Chapter 21

1. What are some of Samuel Clemens's most famous works? (p. 105. Titles mentioned in the first paragraph)

2. The author wants to know: How were the stories of Ben Franklin and Samuel Clemens alike? (p. 106. Both learned printing by working for their older brothers. Neither liked being bossed around, so they left to take printing and writing jobs elsewhere.)

3. The author wants to know: Have you ever dreamed of being somewhere you know you can't really go? (p. 107. After students share their fantasy journeys, you might list the places—real and imaginary—visited by Clemens.)

4. How did Clemens view the Gilded Age? (p. 108. As a time of "ridiculous excess")

Note: See Making Connections for the author's question on page 108.

Making Connections

Use this question to help students link big ideas across chapters. (Suggested responses are in parentheses.)

Imagine that you live in the late 1800s. You have read Shakespeare's description (see page 108) of a gilded age. Do you agree that the description fits the age in which you live? Why or why not? (Answers will vary, but lead students to understand the link between the excesses cited in the verses and the excesses of the late 1800s. Most students will probably agree, citing as the corruption and lavish spending of a Boss Tweed or the hucksterism and generosity of a P.T. Barnum.)

Debating the Issues

The topic below can stimulate debate. (Points to consider are in parentheses.) *Resolved:* That political machines should be outlawed as unconstitutional. (Appoint some students to speak for promachine politicians such as George Washington Plunkitt. Have others speak from the point of view of immigrants who have been helped by the political bosses. Instruct yet other students to represent reformers such as Thomas Nast and Alfred Ely Beach.)

Making Ethical Judgments

The following question asks students to consider issues of ethics. (Points to consider are in parentheses.)

In the caption for the Boss Tweed cartoon on page 95, Thomas Nast asks: "Well, what are you going to do about it?" If you were a voter in New York City in the 1870s, how would you answer that question? (Encourage students to think of ways that citizens can influence political processes—e.g., write letters to honest legislators demanding an investigation, work to elect anticorruption city officials, write letters to the editor, and so on.)

■ PROJECTS AND ACTIVITIES

Writing Captions Refer students to the political cartoon on page 96. Working individually or in small groups, students can write captions expressing the cartoon's message. From these captions, what can students infer about the way(s) in which the Tammany machine built its power? (By paying people for do-nothing jobs)

Interpreting a Political Cartoon Tell students that political cartoonists use a variety of tools to get their messages across. These tools include labels, captions, caricatures, exaggerated features, symbols, etc. Ask students to analyze Nast's use of these tools in the cartoon on page 97.

Linking Past and Present Read aloud the author's question on page 97: Do you hear people complain about politics today? Next, have students brainstorm a list of some of the most commonly heard complaints. Working in groups, students can create political cartoons criticizing one of these situations using Thomas Nast's cartoons as models.

Writing an Obituary Ask students to imagine they are reporters for a New York newspaper. Have them write an obituary for Alfred Ely Beach. The columns should profile Beach's lifetime achievements, including his role in promoting justice.

Designing an Advertisement Have students work in small groups to design posters announcing the arrival of the Barnum and Bailey Circus in a small town on the Midwest prairie. Posters should highlight the attractions of the three-ring circus.

Using Historical Imagination Refer students back to the picture of children playing on the prairie on pages 70–71. Then have them close their eyes as you read aloud the author's description (pages 102–103) of a circus's arrival in town. Assign students to write letters to a friend in which they describe their feelings about the arrival of the circus. (Letters should answer, in part, why they have waited all year for this event.)

Making Oral Book Reports Assign interested students to read one of the books or short stories written by Mark Twain. Have them present the plots to the class in the form of a storytelling session.

■ BRIDGING THE PARTS

Developing Empathy In 1894, a young Russian Jew named Mary Antin recalled her parents' decision to go to America.

So at last I was going to America! The boundaries burst. The arch of heaven soared. A million suns shone out for every star. The winds rushed in from outer space, roaring in my ears, "America! America!"

Request volunteers to suggest adjectives that capture Mary's feelings. Despite political corruption, why might immigrants still see the United States as the "promised land?"

■ STUDY GUIDE

The Study Guide appears on page 53. Guidelines and page references for answers are provided below.

1. (a) pp. 95–97 (schemer) (b) pp. 97–98, 100 (dreamer) (c) p. 99 (schemer) (d) pp. 99–100 (dreamer) (e) pp. 101–104 (both) (f) pp. 105–110 (dreamer)

2. (a) pp. 95–96 (East) (b) p. 105, 109 (Midwest) (c) pp. 106–107 (West) (d) p. 109 (West) Features should reflect text descriptions.

3. (a) p. 95 (b) pp. 95, 97 (c) p. 97 (d) p. 100 (e) p. 100 (f) p. 101 (g) 102 (h) p. 102 (i) p. 108

4. pp. 95–100; (a) that Tweed controlled the voting, thus undermining democracy (b) Beach built a subway "under his nose"; Nast drew cartoons exposing the corruption.

5. p. 99; *Dishonest graft:* blackmailers, gamblers, saloon-keepers, disorderly people. *Honest graft:* making a profit off inside political deals. Both open government to corruption.

6. pp. 101–104; Answers will vary. Encourage students to use colorful language and descriptions of "rare spectacles."

7. pp. 105–110; Answers will vary, but students should cite examples like *Huckleberry Finn* in which the characters are a slave searching for freedom and a boy who loves adventure.

8. Answers will vary. To encourage discussion, ask students what differences they see between how children and adults think. What advantages and disadvantages are there to each way of thinking?

9. Political machines, because they developed a power base and government outside of legitimate political channels. (You might discuss how our two-party system has safeguarded justice through the development of a "loyal opposition" to keep watch on the party in power.)

PART 5
In Search of Liberty (Chapters 22–28)

The Big Ideas

In 1884, the Statue of Liberty arrived in New York Harbor. The gift from France lacked a pedestal, so Hungarian immigrant Joseph Pulitzer used his newspaper to raise the money. Some 120,000 adults and children sent in a small fortune in dimes and nickels. In 1886, when the city set the statue in place, an American Jew named Emma Lazarus donated a poem for its base. Declared the now-famous lines:

Give me your tired, your poor,

Your huddled masses yearning to breathe free,

The wretched refuse of your teeming shore,

Send these, the homeless, tempest-tost, to me:

I lift my lamp beside the golden door. . .

The diversity of people who helped raise the Statue of Liberty was rivaled only by the diversity of people who arrived on United States shores in the late 1800s. Nearly all came in search of freedom—economic, political, and/or religious. Part 5 explores the nation's growing diversity and efforts of reformers to win greater justice for all.

Chapter Summaries

Each of the seven chapters in Part 5 explores the ongoing struggle to realize the promises of liberty and equality held out by the Declaration of Independence. The stories are as follows.

Chapter 22

Immigrants Speak (pp. 111–118)

Although the Germans and Irish made up the largest groups of nineteenth-century immigrants, the late 1800s saw a flood of newcomers from eastern and southern Europe. Their arrival fueled the growth of cities and industry alike, thus propelling the nation into the modern era.

People to Meet John Smith, Carl Schurz, Thomas Nast, Mathilde Franziska Anneke, Abraham Lincoln, Michael Pupin, Bianca de Carli, Jacob Riis, Léon Carles Fouquet

Places to Visit New York City, Ellis Island, St. Louis

Terms to Define tenements, hold, steerage, abysmal, abyss, abyssal

Chapter 23

More About Immigrants (pp. 119–122)

Although most immigrants cherished American ideals, not all Americans welcomed them. The backlash against immigrants took the form of ugly ethnic, racial, and religious prejudice.

People to Meet Xu, Confucius

Place to Visit Pulaski (in Tennessee)

Terms to Define Know-Nothing Party, Ku Klux Klan, anti-Semitic, Workingmen's Party, exploit, Golden Mountain, depression, racism, Chinese Exclusion Act

Chapter 24

The Strange Case of the Chinese Laundry (pp. 123–125)

The Chinese of San Francisco felt the lash of prejudice when white law officials shut down their laundries. The fact that white-owned laundries remained open added extra sting to the injustice.

People to Meet Sheriff Hopkins, Yick Wo, President Hayes

Place to Visit San Francisco

Terms to Define ordinance, naturalized citizen, nativism, Chinese Exclusion Act

Chapter 25

Going to Court (pp. 126–129)

The case of *Yick Wo* v. *Hopkins* revealed the power of the 14th Amendment. In a landmark decision, the Supreme Court used the "equal protection" clause to overturn the decision to shut down Chinese laundries in San Francisco.

People to Meet Lee Yick (Yick Wo), Thomas Nast

Place to Visit San Francisco

Terms to Define appeal, criminal law, civil law, double jeopardy, jury, defendant, prosecutors, witnesses, arbitrarily, aliens, briefs

Chapter 26

Tea in Wyoming (pp. 130–132)

Wyoming led the way in granting the vote to women. When the United States threatened to deny the territory statehood unless it abandoned women's suffrage, a representative declared: "We may stay out of the Union a hundred years, but we will come in with our women."

People to Meet Esther Morris, W.R. Steele, Colonel William H. Bright, Julia Bright, John Campbell, Mary G. Bellamy, Jeanette Rankin, Nellie Taylor Ross, Mildred Rutherford, Susan B. Anthony, Louisa Ann Swain

Places to Visit South Pass City (in Wyoming), Oswego (in New York), Cheyenne (in Wyoming), Salem (in Ohio)

Term to Define milliner

Chapter 27

Are You a Citizen If You Can't Vote? (pp. 133–139)

With suffrage won for black males, women sought to win the vote for themselves. Some reformers, such as Susan B. Anthony, risked arrest and trial for casting trial ballots. Others, such as Belva Lockwood, pushed themselves into law practice so they could defend women's rights more forcefully.

People to Meet Susan B. Anthony, Horace Greeley, Ulysses S. Grant, Julia Grant, Elizabeth Cady Stanton, Lucy Stone, Sojourner Truth, Carry Nation, Henry R. Selden, Olympia Brown, Horace Mann, Myra Colby Bradwell, Belva Ann Lockwood, Clara Barton, Alice Hamilton, Anna J. Cooper, Otelia Cromwell, Charlotte Perkins Gilman, Helen Keller, Millard Fillmore, Judge Ward Hunt, Matthew Lyon, John Adams

Places to Visit Washington, D.C.; Nyack (in New York); Detroit (Michigan); Rochester (in New York)

Terms to Define temperance, benign, farthing

Chapter 28

Mary in the Promised Land (pp. 140–145)

In her autobiography, Mary Antin gave a voice to the hopes, hardships, and fulfilled dreams of many immigrants. For Antin, the United States was indeed *The Promised Land.*

People to Meet Mary Antin, Hayye Dvoshe, Elinore Stewart, Flora Spiegelberger, Miss Carpenter, Bishop Juan Bautista Lamy, Jacob Riis

Places to Visit "the Pale of Settlement," Polotzk (in Russia), Boston, Santa Fe

Terms to Define pale, palings, beyond the pale, *shtetl, rebbe, shul* (synagogue), Torah and Talmud

■ INTRODUCING PART 5

Setting a Context in Space and Time

Using Maps To help students envision the movement of people into the United States during the late 1800s, refer them to the map on page 114. Ask them to identify the three regions that sent the largest number of immigrants. (Northern Europe, Central Europe, Southern Europe) From this map, what can students infer about changes in the United States population at the closing years of the century? (That it was growing; that it was becoming more diverse)

Understanding Change over Time To help students understand changing immigration patterns, refer them to the graph on page 114. Ask them in which years immigration reached its lowest points. (Around 1861 or 1862 and in 1880) What historic events accounted for the drops? (The Civil War and an economic depression) In which decade did immigration reach its peak? (1880s) Tell students that in Part 5 they will learn more about the reasons so many immigrants traveled to the United States at this time.

Setting a Context for Reading

Thinking about the Big Ideas To introduce the concept of diversity, tell students that some people describe the United States as a "mini-United Nations." Ask students what this description means. (That people from all over the world live here) Request volunteers to identify their own national, ethnic, or regional ancestry. (You might start by sharing your own ancestry.) List student responses on the chalkboard. As students work their way through Part 5, have them identify which of the groups listed on the chalkboard arrived in large numbers during the late 1800s. Call on volunteers to investigate the peak years of arrival for other groups not covered in Part 5. (If students consult an almanac, for example, they will find that the 1970s and 1980s were peak years for immigrants from Latin America and Southeast Asia. Africans, on the other hand, arrived in large numbers during the slave-trading years.)

■ DISCUSSING PART 5

Understanding the Chapters

The following questions can serve as a guide to discussing each chapter. (Page references and suggested answers or tips are in parentheses.)

Chapter 22

1. Why would John Smith have welcomed the type of immigrants who came to the United States in the nineteenth century? (p. 111. Because they had the skills to build, farm, and invent)

2. Who were the two largest immigrant groups to come at this time? (pp. 111, 113. The Germans and the Irish)

3. Why did immigrants come to America during the second half of the nineteenth century? (pp. 111–115. To escape political unrest, famine, lack of work, religious persecution, and so on)

4. The author says "it took courage to emigrate." What do you think she meant? (pp. 115–117. Encourage students to consider the hardships of the journey and the difficulties of resettling in a strange land.)

5. The author wants to know: Imagining that you are an immigrant who speaks no English, how do you like it here? (p. 115. Invite students who have faced this situation themselves to share their feelings with the class.)

6. The author wants to know: Do you know what Carl Schurz meant when he said "Equality of rights . . . is the great moral element of a true democracy"? (p. 118. To kick off discussion, repeat a quote by Frederick Douglass: "No man can put a chain about the ankle of his fellow man without at last finding the other end fastened about his own neck."

Ask students what happens to a society when one group is denied equality.)

Chapter 23

1. What were some of the reasons people wanted to restrict immigration? (pp. 119–120. Feared job competition, resented taxes to pay for services to help the newcomers, had prejudice against people from different backgrounds)

2. The author wants to know: What do you think of the name "Know-Nothing Party"? (p. 120. As background, tell students that party members used the name to conceal their activities—i.e., "we know nothing." But in reality they knew nothing about the talents and cultures of immigrants.)

3. The author wants to know: What percentage of the population did the Chinese immigrants form in 1882? (p. 120. They formed 0.6 percent.)

4. (a) What values did Chinese immigrants bring to the United States? (p. 122. The belief in honesty, fairness, and loyalty; the need for a balanced life; respect for learning and the family) (b) Why were they still unwelcome? (p. 120. There was a depression, and the Chinese worked for low wages. Untrue stories and different appearances led to racism.)

Chapter 24

1. Why did many Chinese immigrants set up laundries and restaurants in the mining towns of the West? (pp. 123–124. Because of sexism—most men felt washing clothes and cooking were "women's work"—and because these were businesses that required little capital to begin)

2. How did racism play a part in the decision to shut down laundries in San Francisco? (p. 124. Because officials only applied the ordinance to Chinese laundries)

3. The author wants to know: When officials shut down a laundry owned by a woman, what kind of prejudice was that? (p. 124. Sexism)

Note: See Making Ethical Judgments for the author's questions on page 125.

Chapter 25

1. What was the central question in the case of *Yick Wo* v. *Hopkins?* (p. 126. Did a Chinese immigrant such as Lee Yick have the same rights as if he had been an American citizen?)

2. (a) What types of law cases exist in the United States? (pp. 126–127. Civil cases and criminal cases) (b) What is the difference between them? (p. 127. In a civil case, no criminal laws have been broken.)

3. What type of case was the *Yick Wo* trial? Why? (p. 127. A criminal case, because a San Francisco law had been broken)

4. Why was the *Yick Wo* case so important? (p. 128. It ruled on the right of police to enforce a law arbitrarily. It also decided whether aliens had the same rights as citizens.)

5. Why did Sheriff Hopkins and the states that supported him lose the case? (p. 129. Because the Supreme Court ruled that their actions violated the "equal protection" clause of the 14th Amendment)

Chapter 26

1. What role did Esther Morris play in the suffrage movement? (p. 130–131. She convinced Wyoming legislators in both parties to back a women's suffrage bill.)

2. What splits existed among women over suffrage? (p. 132. Some women were against suffrage. A few believed it might be a trick to expand black voting power.)

3. How did the issue of women's suffrage in the Wyoming Territory affect the nation as a whole? (p. 132. Admission of Wyoming would bring women's suffrage into the Union.)

Chapter 27

1. How do you think Susan B. Anthony might define "justice"? (p. 133. As the right of all citizens to vote, regardless of race, sex, religion, or any other characteristic)

2. Put yourself back in the late 1800s. How would you answer the question "Could a marriage survive if a husband and wife voted for different parties?" (p. 133. Students should understand that voting in a free nation involves acting according to a person's individual conscience. Point out that students take this for granted today, but this was not always the case.)

3. What legal injustices faced women in the late 1800s? (p. 135. Could be taxed, but could not vote; could be arrested, but couldn't serve on a jury)

4. What question was raised in the trial of Susan B. Anthony? (p. 136. If women are citizens, why don't they have the right to vote?)

5. What new issue did the trial raise? (p. 139. The right to a free trial in a free society)

6. The author wants to know: Were the predictions of John Adams cited on page 139 correct? (p. 139. Encourage students to explore the Constitution for amendments that expanded suffrage.)

Note: See Projects and Activities for the author's question on page 137.

Chapter 28

1. Why did Mary Antin's family leave Russia? (pp. 140–142. To escape the poverty and lack of liberty born of religious prejudice)

2. What aspects of life in the United States most pleased the Antins? (pp. 144–145. Right to a free public education; right to live, travel, and work wherever they wanted; the freedom to speak and worship as they pleased)

Making Connections

Use these questions to help students link the big ideas across chapters. (Suggested responses are in parentheses.)

1. How did increased immigration affect prejudice in the late 1800s? (Students should cite examples such as the Know-Nothing Party and the Chinese Exclusion Act, as well as understanding the underlying tensions that fanned racist and nativist sentiments.)

2. What was the link between passage of the 15th Amendment and the women's suffrage movement? (The extension of the vote to black men made women more keenly aware of their own lack of rights as citizens.)

Debating the Issues

The topic below can stimulate debate. (Points to consider are in parentheses.) *Resolved:* That Congress was correct in passing the Chinese Exclusion Act of 1882. (Have some students speak for members of the Know-Nothings. Others might pose as "knowledgeable" economists concerned about the economic depression. Yet others should attack the law citing contributions by the Chinese. Refer this last group to Chapter 13.)

Making Ethical Judgments

The following activity asks students to consider issues of ethics. (Points to consider are in parentheses.)

Suppose you lived in the late 1800s. How would you answer the following questions raised by the author on page 125: "What makes a citizen? Are women citizens?" Now skim through Chapters 22–28. Which individuals would probably share your views? (Answers will vary. Have students support their choices with evidence from the text.)

■ PROJECTS AND ACTIVITIES

Analyzing a Quote Working in small groups, students can rewrite the quote by Carl Schurz on page 112 in their own words. (Encourage students to look up unfamiliar words in the dictionary.) Call on volunteers to read their revisions aloud. Then have them complete the following sentence: "I, Carl Schurz, believe America is the school for liberty because_____."

Identifying Points of View Read the lines by Emma Lazarus on page 34 of this Guide. Then ask students how each of the following might react to these lines: a member of the Know-Nothing Party, Jacob Riis, Mary Antin.

Identifying Prejudice Working in small groups, students can analyze the advertisement on page 121. Ask students to list techniques used by the designer to bias opinion against the Chinese. For example, what does the use of Uncle Sam show? (That it's "patriotic" to kick out the Chinese) Suppose such an ad ran today? How would people react to it? Why?

Conducting Mock Trials Divide the class into two groups. Have one group prepare a mock trial reenacting the case of *Yick Wo* v. *Hopkins*. Have the other group prepare a mock trial of Susan B. Anthony. Instruct lawyers for the defense to state clearly the issues of justice involved in each case. (As a switch, you might have Belva Lockwood defend Anthony.)

Using Historical Imagination As the author requests on page 137, students should imagine that they are President Grant and have received Belva Lockwood's letter. Have them write letters in response.

Designing Historical Posters Have students design posters for Women's History Month, which takes place each year in March. Working individually or in small groups, they can draw posters illustrating the legal and political "firsts" mentioned in Part 5.

■ BRIDGING THE PARTS

Analyzing a Quote In 1887, on the hundredth birthday of the Constitution, President Grover Cleveland declared:

> *Every American citizen should on this centennial day rejoice in their citizenship. . . . He should rejoice because our Constitution . . . has survived so long, and also because . . . [the American people] have demonstrated so fully the strength and value of popular rule.*

Use this quote as a stopping point to assess the meaning of citizenship in 1887. Who enjoyed its benefits? Who did not? Then tell students that Part 6 takes at look at the United States as it enters into the second century of its existence.

■ STUDY GUIDE

The Study Guide appears on page 54. Guidelines and page references for answers are provided below.

1. (a) pp. 111–113, 118 (b) pp. 116, 118 (c) pp. 123–124 (d) pp. 123–124, 126 (e) pp. 130–131 (f) p. 132 (g) pp. 133, 135–136, 138–139 (h) p. 133 (i) p. 137

2. (a) p. 115 (b) 120 (c) pp. 123–125 (d) pp. 130–132 (e) pp. 135–136, 138–139

3. (a) p. 115 (b) pp. 115, 117 (c) p. 121 (d) p. 125 (e) p. 125 (f) p. 128

4. pp. 112–115; Possible responses: Immigration reached an all-time high. Immigrants came from new regions, especially Central and Eastern Europe.

5. Students might refer to some of the conditions cited on pp. 115, 119–120, 142–143.

6. Arguments will vary, but encourage students to mention the violation of rights and issues cited on pp. 123–124, 128.

7. Lee Yick: p. 128. Susan B. Anthony: pp. 135, 138.

8. pp. 130–131. Students should keep in mind the six reporter's questions: *Who? What? When? Where? Why? How?*

9. pp. 144–145. Monologues will vary, but should cite beliefs consistent with Antin's autobiography and age.

10. Answers will vary, but lead students to understand that the belief in ideals such as liberty and equality for all is the thread that holds the American people together.

PART 6
Toward a New Century (Chapters 29–31)

The Big Ideas

To celebrate its one hundredth birthday, the United States organized a grand Centennial Exposition. Explained one pamphlet:

During the past century the progress of the nation in invention and manufactures has been wonderful. . . . To bring together all the evidences of this progress, and to combine in one location the engines of industry and their products, . . . we are to have in the good city of Philadelphia an International Exhibition, to open May 10th, 1876.

For most Americans, the changes since 1776 had been staggering. Many problems still faced the nation. But the "evidences of . . . progress" at the Centennial Exposition convinced many people that the nation might reach for perfection. Part 6 provides a glimpse of the nation at age one hundred.

Chapter Summaries

The three chapters in Part 6 examine the state of the nation on its on hundredth birthday. Stories are as follows.

Chapter 29

100 Candles (pp. 146–150)

The Centennial Exposition celebrated American ingenuity and inventiveness. The marvels unveiled at the fair foreshadowed even greater achievements to come.

People to Meet John Adams, Mrs. E.D. Gillespie, William Dean Howells, George Henry Corliss, President Grant, Alexander Graham Bell

Place to Visit Philadelphi

Terms to Define "consent of the governed," centennial, exposition

Chapter 30

How Were Things in 1876? (pp. 151–153)

The ideal of "equality for all" still lay beyond the reach of many Americans. But the fact that the Constitution had endured the test of civil war convinced most people that the United States would continue to change for the better.

People to Meet William K. Vanderbilt, Mr. and Mrs. Cornelius Vanderbilt, Elizabeth Cady Stanton, Susan B. Anthony, James Hazen Hyde, Walter Camp

Place to Visit Newport (in Rhode Island)

Terms to Define exports, imports, stagnating, middle class

Chapter 31

The Wizard of Electricity (pp. 154–159)

The "invention factory" of Thomas Alva Edison set the pace of change as the nation entered its second century. Edison combined genius with hard work to give Americans phonographs, moving pictures, electricity, and more.

People to Meet Thomas Alva Edison; Mina, Marion, Thomas, Jr., and Theodore Edison; Moses Farmer; Grosvenor Porter Lowrey; J.P. Morgan; Charles Brush; Mary Stilwell

Places to Visit Menlo Park (in New Jersey), Salem (in Massachusetts), Hudson River, New York City, Litchfield (in Minnesota)

Terms to Define mimeograph, filament

■ INTRODUCING PART 6

Setting a Context in Space and Time

Using Maps Ask volunteers to use an opaque projector to draw a large outline map of the United States on posterboard. Have students label the states that made up the Union in 1876, its one hundredth birthday.

Using a Time Line Refer students to the time line on pages 156–157. Suppose the ghost of the one nation's founders revisited the nation on its one hundredth birthday. What changes might be the most surprising? Why?

Setting a Context for Reading

Thinking about the Big Ideas You might begin discussion of Part 6 by writing the word *change* on the chalkboard. Conduct a brainstorming session in which students name all the changes that have taken place in the United States between 1776 and 1876. When students are done, distinguish positive and negative changes. If students had lived in 1876, which two changes might have given them the most pride?

■ DISCUSSING PART 6

Understanding the Chapters

The following questions can serve as a guide to discussing each chapter. (Page references and suggested answers or tips are in parentheses.)

Chapter 29

1. What were some of the reasons that people were excited about the nation's one hundredth birthday? (p. 146. The success of this unique experiment in self-government, surviving a civil war, a thriving nation)

2. What was one of the purposes of the Women's Building? (p. 147. To show that women's inventiveness and artistry went beyond needle and thread)

3. The author wants to know: Besides inventions and material things, what had America achieved in its first hundred years? (p. 150. Answers will vary, but encourage students the think of ways in which liberty and justice had grown.)

Chapter 30

1. In 1876, what were some of the things in which Americans could take pride? (p. 151–152. Free government, Constitution, the end of slavery, growing population and trade, written guarantees of justice such as the 14th Amendment.)

2. What were some of the problems facing the nation? (pp. 152–153. Students should cite injustices such as state-supported inequality, lack of the vote for women, huge income gaps, etc.)

Chapter 31

1. How did Thomas Alva Edison turn disadvantages to advantages? (p. 154. Lack of school caused him to do things for himself; deafness allowed him to concentrate.)

2. What were some of the new ideas to come out of Edison's "invention factory"? (pp. 155–156. Students should describe any of the items mentioned on these two pages.)

3. The author wants to know: Would you lend money to a rumpled young man who said he could light a city? (pp. 157–158. You might use this question to explore the risk side of free enterprise. What would investors have to gain or lose?)

Making Connections

Use the question below to help students link the big ideas across the chapters. (Suggested responses appear in parentheses.)

What was the connection between the growth of technology in the late 1800s and the American belief in progress? (Inventions proved that the nation was moving ahead. Many people believed other areas of life would improve too.)

Debating the Issues

The following topic can stimulate debate. (Points to consider are in parentheses.) *Resolved:* That people should boycott the Centennial Exposition in protest of the lack of rights suffered by some Americans. (Some students can speak for the blacks and women who still failed to enjoy equality. Others should defend the Centennial as a celebration of what the nation has accomplished thus far.)

Making Ethical Judgments

The following question asks students to consider issues of ethics. (Points to consider are in parentheses.)

Suppose you are a very rich person in 1876. What, if any, responsibilities do you have toward helping the poor? (This is a tough question. Encourage students to debate the responsibilities that the privileged have toward the less privileged.)

■ PROJECTS AND ACTIVITIES

Analyzing a Quote In 1833, the chief of the Patent Office resigned, saying: "Everything seems to have been done. I just don't see how anything else can be invented." Ask students why this official would have been surprised by the Centennial Exposition.

Illustrating an Idea To show inequalities in United States life in 1876, have students draw posters entitled "The Two Faces of America." Posters might show freedoms enjoyed by some people and not by others, or they might focus on gaps between rich and poor.

Writing a News Story Challenge students to imagine they are foreign reporters on the day Thomas Edison switched on the lights in New York City. Assign them to write a news story on this latest triumph of "Yankee ingenuity."

■ BRIDGING THE PARTS

Analyzing a Quote Not long after the Civil War ended, the governor of Indiana commented on the treatment of blacks in the North.

We not only exclude them from voting, we exclude them from testifying in courts of justice. We exclude them from our public schools, and we make it unlawful . . . for them to come into the state.

Read this quote aloud, without identifying the geographic background of the speaker. Ask students whether they think the speaker was from the North or South. Use this activity to lead into a discussion of the widespread prejudice against blacks in the late 1800s.

■ STUDY GUIDE

The Study Guide appears on page 55. Guidelines and page references for answers are provided below.

1. (a) p. 147 (b) p. 150 (c) p. 150 (d) p. 152 (e) p. 153 (f) pp. 154–159 (g) p. 158

2. (a) p. 146 (b) p. 155 (c) p. 159

3. (a) p. 146 (b) p. 146 (c) p. 146 (d) p. 151 (e) p. 153 (f) p. 157

4. Speeches will vary, but they will probably emphasize positive achievements.

5. Answers will vary. But students might mention specific displays.

6. pp. 151–153; That the ways of life between two classes vary dramatically

7. Answers will vary, but most people at the time expressed shock, then anger.

8. Answers will vary, but you might encourage students to think of the qualities that might make a successful inventor.

9. p. 159; That genius results from a lot of hard work. You might organize a class debate on whether, in fact, hard work without genius is enough or vice versa.

10. Because of the nature of the Centennial, most changes will center on technological advancements.

PART 7
The Unfinished Journey (Chapters 32–37)

The Big Ideas

In 1897, a professor at Atlanta University named W.E.B. DuBois delivered a civil rights speech. Said DuBois:

[A]n American, a Negro, two souls, two thoughts, two unreconciled strivings. . . . The history of the American Negro is the history of this strife. . . . He would not bleach the Negro soul in a flood of white Americanism. . . . He simply wishes to make it possible for a man to be both a Negro and an American, without being cursed.

With African Americans bowing under the heavy hand of Jim Crow, DuBois called upon African Americans to claim their dual heritage. He demanded justice amid a time of segregation and lynchings. Not all African Americans agreed with DuBois. But his ideas planted seeds that would bear fruit at a later time. Part 7 describes the laws and practices that sought to crush the African American spirit and the people who worked to inspire black dignity amid this crisis.

Chapter Summaries

The six chapters in Part 7 provide a sweeping look at the Jim Crow era and at three prominent figures of that time—Ida B. Wells, Booker T. Washington, and W.E.B. DuBois. The stories are as follows.

Chapter 32
Jim Crow—What a Fool! (pp. 160–164)

Hopes of equality from Reconstruction were dashed by the decision in *Plessy* v. *Ferguson.* The only victor in the case was a vaudeville-inspired fool named Jim Crow.

People to Meet Jim Crow, Frederick Douglass, Homer Plessy, John H. Ferguson, John Marshall Harlan

Places to Visit Charleston, New Orleans, Chicago

Terms to Define segregation, Jim Crow, black codes, Redeemers, voter fraud, franchise, poll tax, white supremacy, Holocaust, lynched, *Plessy* v. *Ferguson,* executive branch, legislative branch, judicial branch, judicial review

Chapter 33
Ida B. Wells (pp. 165–169)

Ida B. Wells shouldered responsibility at an early age—not only for her family, but for the African American struggle for equality. Even at threat of death, she refused to abandon the struggle for justice.

People to Meet Ida B. Wells, O.O. Howard, Jim and Lizzie Wells, Elizabeth Warrenton, Dr. Samuel Mudd, John Wilkes Booth, President Andrew Johnson, President William McKinley, Mary Ann Shadd Cary, Thomas Fortune, Isaiah Montgomery, Mary Virginia Montgomery

Places to Visit Holly Springs (in Mississippi), Norfolk (in Virginia), Dry Tortugas, London, Memphis, Mound Bayou (in Mississippi)

Chapter 34
Lynching Means Killing by a Mob (pp. 170–173)

After slavery, one of the darkest blots on our history was the era in which vigilante justice killed thousands of innocent people. To effect change, Ida B. Wells championed the passage of antilynching laws.

People to Meet Ida B. Wells, Thomas Moss, Charles Russell, Charles Lynch, Thomas Fortune, Ferdinand Barnett

Place to Visit Memphis

Terms to Define lynching, vigilante justice, anarchy

Chapter 35

A Man and His Times (pp. 174–176)

Booker T. Washington placed economic freedom ahead of other types of freedom. His judgment grew out of the times in which he lived—a time in which many African Americans in the South barely scratched a living from the land.

People to Meet Booker T. Washington, Arthur M. Schlesinger, Jr., George Washington Carver

Places to Visit Franklin County (in Virginia), Hampton (in Virginia), Tuskegee (in Alabama)

Chapter 36

A Man Ahead of His Times (pp. 177–180)

W.E.B. DuBois rejected Booker T. Washington's approach to change. In words similar to those of the civil rights movement of the 1950s and 1960s, DuBois demanded nothing less than full equality.

People to Meet Booker T. Washington, William Edward Burghardt (W.E.B.) DuBois, President Theodore Roosevelt, Andrew Carnegie, John D. Rockefeller, Carl Schurz, Dudley Randall

Places to Visit Great Barrington (in Massachusetts), Niagara Falls

Terms to Define anti-Semitism, National Association for the Advancement of Colored People (NAACP)

Chapter 37

End Words (pp. 181–183)

Although America was far from perfect at the end of the nineteenth century, it was headed in the direction of freedom and equality for all of its citizens.

People to Meet Thomas Jefferson, John Adams, Benjamin Franklin, Roger Williams, William Penn, James Oglethorpe, Tucker brothers, Jakob Mithelstadt, Andrew Jackson, Abraham Lincoln, Elizabeth Cady Stanton, Susan B. Anthony, Thaddeus Stevens, Ida B. Wells, Mary Antin, Irving Berlin, George Gershwin, Aaron Copland, Leonard Bernstein, Carl Schurz, Gerhard Gesell, Arnold Gesell

■ INTRODUCING PART 7

Setting a Context in Space and Time

Interpreting Historical Maps Tell students that between the years 1882 and 1958, mob murders, or executions without benefit of trial, were reported in every state in the Union except Rhode Island, Connecticut, New Hampshire, and Massachusetts. The following statistics concern those states in which more than fifty percent of the mob murders were committed against African Americans.

Mob Murders	
Number	*States*
1–9	NY, PA, NJ, DE
10–49	WV, MD, OH, IL
50–199	MO, VA, NC, SC
200–399	FL, AL, TN, KY, AR, LA
400 or more	TX, MS, GA

Source: Historical Atlas of the United States (National Geographic)

Distribute copies of these figures, and have students use them to key in an outline map of the United States. Ask students in which region African Americans were at the greatest risk of violence. (The South) Were African Americans safe in the North? (Not really) From this map, what can students infer about violence against African Americans in the years between Reconstruction and the Civil Rights Movement? (That it was widespread)

Forming Chronological Inferences Refer students to the Chronology on page 184. Tell them to examine the dates for the years after the end of Reconstruction (1876). How might black Americans have described these years? (As years in which they suffered injustices) Encourage students to name specific events that support their inferences.

Setting a Context for Reading You might open discussion by writing the title of Part 7 on the chalkboard: The Unfinished Journey. Have students skim through the six chapters that make up the final portion of the book. With whose journey is Part 7 mainly concerned? (The journey of African Americans) If the journey of African Americans was unfinished, what can students infer about the journey of the entire nation? (That it too was unfinished) Use this discussion to lead students to understand that the nation's strivings for perfection would not end until all its peoples enjoyed equal justice.

■ DISCUSSING PART 7

Understanding the Chapters

The following questions can serve as a guide to discussing each chapter. (Page references and suggested answers or tips are in parentheses.)

Chapter 32

1. What were race relations like in the North and South before the Civil War? (pp. 160–161. *North:* no slavery, segregation; *South:* slavery, no segregation)

2. By the end of Reconstruction, how had these relations changed? (p. 161. *North:* segregation by habit continued. *South:* segregation backed up by law and violence began.)

3. The author wants to know: What does "equal protection of the laws" mean? (p. 162. That all the laws apply equally to all people)

4. The author wants to know: Were the Jim Crow laws constitutional or unconstitutional? What about laws and taxes that prevented blacks from voting? (pp. 162–163. Help students use provisions from the 14th and 15th amendments in their decisions.)

5. (a) What was the issue in the case of *Plessy* v. *Ferguson.* (p. 163. Whether "separate but equal" laws were constitutional) (b) What did the court rule? (p. 163. It upheld these laws, opening the way for legal segregation.)

Chapter 33

1. What character traits describe Ida B. Wells as a teenager? (pp. 165–167. Courageous, honest, responsible, etc.)

2. How did Wells respond to segregation when she moved to Memphis? (p. 169. She fought it, physically and in a court of law.)

3. What was an "Understanding Law"? (p. 169. A law requiring voters to demonstrate that they could understand the Constitution; a tool to limit the voting rights of blacks)

4. How did Isaiah Montgomery respond to this law? Why? (p. 169. He went along with it so as to gain more influence among whites.)

Chapter 34

1. How did vigilante justice violate the 14th Amendment? (pp. 170–171. Deprived victims of due process of law—the right to a fair trial.

2. How would this type of justice affect a society? (p. 171. It would produce little more than anarchy.)

3. What actions did Ida B. Wells take to protest lynchings? (pp. 172–173. Wrote about them, organized boycotts)

4. What was the price of her courage? (p. 172. Her press was wrecked, and her life was threatened.)

Note: See Making Ethical Judgments for the author's question on page 172.

Chapter 35

1. What obstacle did Booker T. Washington overcome to gain an education? (p. 174. The poverty of a former slave)

2. What example did he set for other people? (p. 175. The value of hard work)

3. The author wants to know: Do you think that statement (by Booker T. Washington, page 175) was wise or foolish? (There is no

right or wrong answer to this question. Some students may feel Washington took the most practical course, given the extreme prejudice at the time. Others may feel that change would never come unless African Americans took stands like that of Ida B. Wells.)

4. What advice did Booker T. Washington offer black students at Tuskegee? (p. 176. To win economic freedom before battling for other freedoms.)

Chapter 36

1. How did Booker T. Washington approach relations with white Americans? (p. 178. He compromised with them on matters of prejudice.)

2. How did W.E.B. DuBois differ in his relations with whites? (pp. 178–179. He refused to compromise with anyone on the matter of equality.)

3. How did W.E.B. DuBois's childhood experiences compare with those of Booker T. Washington? (p. 179. He grew up free amid the democracy of New England town meetings. He learned pride in his African heritage from his grandfather and enjoyed the prestige of a Harvard education.)

4. DuBois wondered whether African Americans could be both African *and* black. What did he decide? (pp. 179–180. That blacks had a double heritage that enriched the nation)

5. The author wants to know: What did DuBois mean when he said "Responsibility is the first step in responsibility"? (p. 180. That people learn responsibility only by being given the chance—and the right—to act responsibly.)

Note: See Debating the Issues and Making Ethical Judgments for the author's questions on pages 178 and 180.

Chapter 37

1. What tools did the nation's founders give us for perfecting the nation? (p. 181. The ideals in the Declaration of Independence.)

2. What were some of the "layers of democracy" that later generations added to the promise of freedom? (pp. 182–183. You might give students the option of answering this question in written form or of presenting the answer in the form of an "idea pyramid." The promises of the Declaration can form the base, with other advances forming new levels reaching for the pinnacle, or perfection.)

Making Connections

Use the questions below to link the big ideas across the chapters. (Suggested responses appear in parentheses.)

1. Who do you think Ida B. Wells might be most likely support—Booker T. Washington or W.E.B. DuBois? Why? (Probably DuBois, because of his activist approach to change.)

2. What was the connection between *Plessy* v. *Ferguson* and the spread of injustices against African Americans? (It institutionalized segregation in the United States and redefined the 14th Amendment.)

Debating the Issues

The topic below can stimulate debate. (Points to consider are in parentheses.) *Resolved:* That Booker T. Washington was right in compromising with whites until black Americans gained more economic clout. (The debate should include the voices of Washington, Wells, DuBois, and Montgomery. To heat up the debate even more, you might appoint a few white spokespersons such as Andrew Carnegie.)

Making Ethical Judgments

The following questions ask students to consider issues of ethics. (Points to consider are in parentheses.)

1. Put yourself in the shoes of Isaiah Montgomery. Given the backlash against blacks in Mississippi, would you have opposed the "Understanding Law"? (Answers will vary, but have students weigh the force of hatred that blacks faced at the time.)

2. On page 172, the author asks whether there are times when people should take the law into their own hands. Why or why not? (First discuss vigilante justice. Then look at alternatives, e.g., the citizen's arrest, the good samaritan, the use of the 911 number.)

3. On page 180, the author asks what happens to you when you hate somebody. (After students express their feelings about hatred, discuss the difficulty of not hating when faced by prejudice. Ask students to analyze the effect on themselves when they feel hatred for someone or something.)

■ PROJECTS AND ACTIVITIES

Showing Reasoned Judgment Frederick Douglass urged black Southerners not to flee the Jim Crow South. "[G]oing into a strange land," he said, "is a confession . . . [that] equal rights and equal protection in any State . . . may be struck down by violence." Tell students to imagine they are black Southerners in 1880. Working in small groups, students should decide whether they will heed Douglass's advice or escape the repression.

Designing a Flowchart To illustrate the process of judicial review, students can design a flowchart showing the way in which the case of *Plessy* v. *Ferguson* reached the Supreme Court.

Using Primary Sources Ask students to write a brief biography of Ida B. Wells that might appear in a book called *Crusaders for Justice*. Have them base their work on the quotations in Chapters 33 and 34.

Designing Posters A slogan in the Memphis streetcar boycott organized by Wells read: "Do not trample on our pride by being 'jim crowed.' Walk!" Request volunteers to design posters illustrating this slogan.

Digging Deeper The author wanted to include a chapter on George Washington Carver in the book—but there wasn't room. Have interested students write this chapter for her. Distribute copies to the class.

■ BRIDGING THE BOOKS

Making Predictions End this book with a discussion of challenges the nation will face as it heads into the modern era. To kick off discussion, read this quote from Teddy Roosevelt's 1905 inaugural address.

Such growth in wealth, in population, and in power as this nation has seen . . . is inevitably accompanied by a like growth in the problems which are ever before a nation that rises to greatness.

Ask students what new issues the nation might have to tackle as it becomes an urban industrial nation. What issues might arise as it becomes a world power?

■ STUDY GUIDE

The Study Guide appears on page 56. Guidelines and page references are provided below.

1. (a) p. 163 (b) p. 164 (c) pp. 165–173 (d) pp. 174–176 (e) pp. 178–180

2. (a) pp. 165–167 (b) p. 175 (c) pp. 175–176 (d) p. 179 (e) p. 179

3. (a) pp. 160–161 (b) p. 161 (c) p. 161 (d) p. 162 (e) p. 163 (f) pp. 170–171

4. pp. 170–172; Paragraphs will vary, but students should stress that lynching violated the most basic principles of "due process."

5. p. 176; Letters will vary, but students should capture some of the practical nature of instruction as well as the creativity of the research done by Carver.

6. pp. 174–176; Because Washington was reacting to the very real poverty and deep-rooted prejudices of his era

7. pp. 177–180; Because DuBois anticipated the civil rights movement of the 1950s and 1960s.

8. pp. 178–180; DuBois felt that no avenue should be closed to people and that to start at the bottom was to accept white prejudice.

9. p. 164; as something enjoyed equally by people of all races and classes

10. Answers will vary, but should focus on the realization of the promises in the 14th and 15th amendments.

Summarizing Book Seven

■ DISCUSSING THE BIG IDEAS

Use the following questions to help students pull together some of the major concepts and themes covered in this book. (Suggested responses or tips are in parentheses.) Note: You may wish to assign these as essay questions for assessment.

1. What changes did Radical Republicans try to bring to the South? Which, if any, of these changes succeeded? (Students should focus on efforts to reshape southern society from the bottom up. First and foremost, the Radicals wanted to give power to black Southerners and take it from former Confederates. Although Reconstruction largely failed in the late 1800s, the 14th and 15th amendments gave future generations the tools to bring about more long-lasting changes.)

2. In 1906, Senator Benjamin Tillman of South Carolina stood to address the Senate. The subject was the end of Reconstruction. Said Tillman:

> *It was in 1876, thirty years ago. . . . Life ceased to be worth having on the terms under which we were living. . . . [I]n desperation, we determined to take the government away from blacks.*

What techniques did white Southerners such as Tillman use "to take government away from the blacks"? (Techniques include vigilante justice, voter fraud, use of poll taxes and literacy tests, and so on.) Suppose you were a black senator from the South. How would you describe the same period in history? (A black Senator might also say life "ceased to be worth having." However, the reasons would center on the injustices of raw terror and Jim Crow.)

3. In 1870, a Dakota newspaper boasted: "Without the railroad it would have required a century to accomplish what has been done in five years." How would each of the following describe the changes brought by the railroad: (a) a Native American,

Note from the Author

History is a natural with children. It is—or should be—all about people and ideas and adventures. That we have made it dull is the wonder.

(b) a cattleherder, (c) a homesteader? (Answers will vary. But for Native Americans, the railroad meant destruction of the buffalo, a flood of settlers, and the end of a way of life. For a cattleherder, the railroad also ended a way of life as trains eliminated the long drives. For homesteaders, the railroads offered a route west and, in many cases, cheap land.)

4. Mark Twain once said: "Nothing so much needs reforming as other people's habits." If you lived during the Gilded Age, which people's habits would you have most wanted to reform? Why? (Answers will vary. Choices might include corrupt politicians such as Boss Tweed, lavish spenders such as William Vanderbilt, and so on.)

5. What factors helped push immigrants out of Europe and Asia? What factors pulled them toward the United States? (*Push:* warfare, lack of religious freedom, poverty, famine, etc. *Pull:* Stable government, religious freedom, economic opportunity, and ideals such as liberty and equality.)

6. Imagine you are a student in 1876. Your teacher has just told you about a writing contest in celebration of the Centennial. The object is to write an essay or poem honoring the growth of American justice. The prize is a free trip to the Centennial Exposition. What information will you include in your essay or poem? (Answers will vary, but students might touch on some of the points mentioned in Chapter 37.)

7. Compare the ideas of Ida B. Wells, Booker T. Washington, and W.E.B. DuBois. What goal did all three of these African American leaders share? How did they differ in their methods of achieving this goal? (All three worked to win better lives for African Americans. To win economic advancement, Washington was willing to compromise until whites learned to give up their prejudice. Neither Wells nor DuBois accepted compromise when it came to issues of civil rights.)

■ SUGGESTIONS FOR ASSESSMENT

You may wish to use the Study Guides on pages 50–56 to assess student learning for each Part. Additional suggestions for assessment appear below. (These activities are tied to ongoing projects suggested on pages 10–11 of this Guide.)

Using Parallel Time Lines When students have completed their parallel time lines, ask them to compare progress in the South with progress in the rest of the nation. Do items on the time lines support the following claim by the author (page 152): "The South [paid for] state-supported inequality . . . by stagnating"? Why or why not?

Using Maps Assign students to review their maps. Suppose they had worked for the U.S. Census in 1880. What three important population patterns would they report?

Editing Historical Writing When students have finished their own history books for Book Seven, have them exchange their books with other students. Challenge students to pick one or two chapters in their classmates' books for editing. On a separate sheet of

paper, students can list suggestions for needed clarifications or other improvements. They should also note well-written or especially interesting selections. Student editors should meet with "authors" to discuss the changes. After "authors" have revised their work, call on volunteers to read their revised chapters aloud. Encourage them to note tips that helped improve their writing.

Teaching History If students have acted as teachers for the class, ask them to evaluate their own teaching techniques: What worked best; what they would do differently the next time?

Mastering the Facts With students, set up a version of a game, such as Jeopardy, in which they test their mastery of items recorded in the class reference books (see page 11 of this Guide). Some students, for example, can make cards with the names of people, places, or terms. Every time a card is held up, students on competing teams must raise their hands and form questions that use the name or word correctly. If they misuse any item or fail to respond, have students consult the appropriate reference source.

Note from the Author

I like to ask children to write their own tests. They have to think to do that. Then I have them answer their own questions and someone else's as well.

Study Guide

PART 1

The Agony of Reconstruction (Chapters 1-7)

Answering the following questions will help you understand and remember what you have read in Chapters 1 to 7. Write your answers on a separate sheet of paper.

1. The people listed below played a part in shaping the direction of Reconstruction. Tell who each person was and how he or she took part in Reconstruction.
   a. Abraham Lincoln
   b. Andrew Johnson
   c. Mary Peake
   d. Charlotte Forten
   e. Blanche Bruce
   f. Hiram Revels
   g. Thaddeus Stevens
   h. Edmund G. Ross

2. As you know, the Civil War took place mostly in the South. So did Reconstruction. Imagine you are a federal agent visiting each of the following places at the times mentioned. Write down any problems that you might observe. Also note any activities that promote rebuilding of the region.
   a. Charleston, 1865
   b. Memphis and New Orleans, 1865–1866
   c. Port Royal, South Carolina, 1865–1866
   d. Atlanta, 1867–1870

3. Define each of the following terms. Then explain its significance to events of the time.
   a. Freedmen's Bureau
   b. martial law
   c. military Reconstruction
   d. carpetbaggers
   e. scalawags
   f. impeachment

4. In 1870, the U.S. Census Bureau would find a larger nation—both in terms of physical size and population. How were people and land added to the United States during the 1860s?

5. During Reconstruction, an African American said: "It seemed like it took a long time for freedom to come. Everything just kept on like it was." How did each of the following work against change in the South?
   a. Ku Klux Klan
   b. black codes
   c. race riots

6. List the provisions of the Reconstruction Act. How do you think each of the following people would have responded to these provisions: (a) a carpetbagger, (b) a scalawag, (c) a freedman or freed woman, (d) a former Confederate officer? Explain your reasons for each answer.

7. Suppose you had been Thaddeus Stevens. What arguments would you have used to convince members of Congress to support impeachment proceedings?

8. Do you think that Johnson had a fair trial in the Senate? What evidence in the text supports your opinion?

9. Imagine you are the editor of an African American newspaper. Write an obituary on the death of Thaddeus Stevens.

10. *Thinking about the Big Ideas:* How did the 14th Amendment extend justice in the United States? How did it change the structure of United States government? How did it provide a tool for bringing about change in the decades ahead?

Study Guide

PART 2

Retreat from the South (Chapters 8–10)

Answering the following questions will help you understand and remember what you have read in Chapters 8 to 10. Write your answers on a separate sheet of paper.

1. Suppose you are an author writing a historical narrative entitled "The Final Days of Reconstruction." Identify each of the following people. Then tell why he or she is important to your story.
   a. Robert Brown Elliot
   b. Jonathan C. Gibbs
   c. Mary Virginia Montgomery
   d. Jefferson Davis
   e. Ulysses S. Grant
   f. Wade Hampton
   g. Rutherford B. Hayes

2. You must also pick geographic settings for your book. What events related to Reconstruction took place at each of the following sites?
   a. Charleston, South Carolina
   b. Fort Monroe, Virginia
   c. Davis Bend
   d. Mound Bayou

3. Define each of these terms. Then explain how the term relates to the final years of Reconstruction.
   a. sharecropping
   b. poll tax
   c. lynching
   d. segregation
   e. redeemers

4. Some people describe the South Carolina constitutional convention as the start of "America's Second Revolution." What was so revolutionary about this meeting?

5. Write an advertisement that Benjamin Montgomery might have written to attract laborers to Davis Bend.

6. Suppose the Montgomery family hired you to defend their property rights at Davis Bend. What arguments would you use to challenge claims by Jefferson Davis? What does Davis's victory tell you about the rights of black Southerners in the late 1870s?

7. How did Ulysses S. Grant earn the nick name of Useless S. Grant?

8. How did the provisions of the 13th, 14th, and 15th amendments allow later reformers to challenge the following practices?
   a. poll taxes
   b. segregated railroad cars
   c. lynchings

9. ***Thinking about the Big Ideas:*** The author says that in the second half of the twentieth century a black minister would heal the old wounds and begin real Reconstruction in America. Who was that minister? (If you need a clue, look at the national holidays celebrated in the month of January.)

10. ***Thinking about the Big Ideas:*** How did Reconstruction legislatures attempt to increase justice in the South? Which of the changes sought by these governments are part of our life today?

RECONSTRUCTION AND REFORM

Study Guide

PART 3

Battle for the West (Chapters 11–18)

Answering the following questions will help you understand and remember what you have read in Chapters 11 to 18. Write your answers on a separate sheet of paper.

1. The people listed below played a part in this period of our history. Tell who each person was and what he or she did of importance.
   a. John Wesley Powell
   b. Elijah G. McCoy
   c. Joseph G. McCoy
   d. Jesse Chisholm
   e. Nat Love
   f. Elizabeth E. Johnson
   g. Leland Stanford
   h. George Pullman
   i. Willa Cather
   j. Cyrus McCormick
   k. George Washington Carver
   l. Crazy Horse
   m. Chief Joseph

2. What happened at each of these places? How were these events connected with the loss of Native American lands and cultures?
   a. Oklahoma Territory
   b. Promontory Point, Utah
   c. Little Big Horn River
   d. Pine Ridge Agency School, Dakota Territory
   e. Wounded Knee

3. Define each of these terms. Then explain its significance to the events of the time.
   a. capital
   b. Texas longhorns
   c. ties
   d. subsidy
   e. emigrant cars
   f. Homestead Act
   g. barbed wire
   h. prairie
   i. Morrill Act
   j. reservations

4. Suppose you were a member of one of the Plains peoples such as the Cheyenne or Sioux. How would you describe the Great Plains? Now suppose you were a homesteader. How would you describe the same land?

5. Write diary entries describing a typical cattle drive up the Chisholm Trail. Include descriptions of both the hardships and rewards of working the open range.

6. When the Union Pacific and the Central Pacific met, reporters from all over the country sent telegraph messages into their home offices. Write a twenty-five-word message that you might have sent on this historic occasion.

7. Write an advertisement that Joseph Glidden might have designed to convince homesteaders to buy his new product, barbed wire.

8. How did the wide-open geography of the Plains encourage the rise of commercial farming?

9. ***Thinking about the Big Ideas:*** Recall the speech by Chief Joseph after the United States government confined the Nez Perce to a land-poor reservation. How would Chief Joseph define the term *justice?*

10. ***Thinking about the Big Ideas:*** How did settlement of the Plains bring changes to Native Americans and to the nation as a whole?

Study Guide

PART 4

Schemers and Dreamers (Chapters 19–21)

Answering the following questions will help you understand and remember what you have read in Chapters 19 to 21. Write your answers on a separate sheet of paper.

1. The people listed below played a key role in the events described in these chapters. Identify each person. Then tell whether each was a "schemer," a "dreamer," or both. Give reasons to support your choices.
   a. William Marcy Tweed
   b. Alfred Ely Beach
   c. George Washington Plunkitt
   d. Thomas Nast
   e. Phineas T. Barnum
   f. Mark Twain

2. The United States was a very diverse place by the late 1800s. Name the region in which each of the following places was located, and tell what the place was like at the time.
   a. New York City
   b. Hannibal, Missouri
   c. San Francisco, California
   d. Crede, Colorado

3. Define each of these terms. Then explain its significance to the events of the time.
   a. graft
   b. Tammany Hall
   c. political machines
   d. constituents
   e. fraud
   f. humbug
   g. robber barons
   h. reformers
   i. Gilded Age

4. When he was accused of corruption, Boss Tweed remarked: "As long as I count the votes, what are you going to do about it?"

(a) What insight does this give you into injustices at the time? (b) How did reformers call Tweed's bluff?

5. According to George Washington Plunkitt, what was the difference between "dishonest graft" and "honest graft"? Why is all graft a threat to democratic government?

6. Imagine you are P.T. Barnum. You have decided to act as ring master on the opening night of your all-new three-ring circus. Write a brief speech announcing the lineup of events. (Keep in mind Barnum's own advice: "I saw everything depended on getting people to think, and talk, and become curious and excited over and about the 'rare spectacle.'")

7. The author says that Mark Twain made Americans think about who we are and what we want to be. How do you think his books do that?

8. The author says that even in old age Mark Twain "could still think like a child, which isn't a bad thing." What do you think she meant?

9. **Thinking about the Big Ideas:** The framers of the Constitution failed to foresee two political changes—the development of political parties and the rise of political machines. Which posed the greater threat to justice? Explain.

Study Guide

PART 5

In Search of Liberty (Chapters 22–28)

Answering the following questions will help you understand and remember what you have read in Chapters 22 to 28. Write your answers on a separate sheet of paper.

1. The people listed below each had his or her own ideas on liberty and justice in the United States. Identify each person. Then tell how each one viewed these ideals.
   a. Carl Schurz
   b. Jacob Riis
   c. Sheriff Hopkins
   d. Lee Yick (Yick Wo)
   e. Esther Morris
   f. Mildred Rutherford
   g. Susan B. Anthony
   h. Horace Greeley
   i. Belva Ann Lockwood

2. Each of the following places is related to the growth of United States diversity in some way. Tell what each place was and explain its link to diversity.
   a. Ellis Island
   b. Pulaski, Tennessee
   c. San Francisco
   d. Wyoming
   e. Rochester, New York

3. Define each of these terms. Then explain its significance to the events of the time.
   a. tenements
   b. steerage
   c. Golden Mountain
   d. nativism
   e. Chinese Exclusion Act
   f. aliens

4. Suppose you are a worker for the U.S. Census Bureau in 1890. Your job is to summarize the major changes in immigration in the past decade. What changes will you cite?

5. Near the end of the century, a Polish immigrant decided to return to Europe. Explained the woman: "We are going back to the Old Country. America ne dobre [not good]. . . . The air ne dobre, the food ne dobre, the houses ne dobre." What living conditions faced by many immigrants might help explain her words?

6. Suppose you are Lee Yick. What arguments will you use to convince other Chinese laundry owners to join you in a suit against the city of San Francisco?

7. How were the 14th and 15th amendments linked to the trials of Lee Yick and Susan B. Anthony?

8. Imagine you are a reporter for an eastern paper such as *The New York Times*. Write a brief news article on the Wyoming Tea Party.

9. Put yourself in Mary Antin's shoes on her first day at Boston's Latin School. Write a monologue that captures your private thoughts as you start elementary school in the United States.

10. ***Thinking about the Big Ideas:*** List some of the ideals that attracted immigrants to the United States. Then explain how these ideals helped unite the diverse peoples who came to this nation in the late 1800s.

Study Guide

PART 6

Toward a New Century (Chapters 29–31)

Answering the following questions will help you understand and remember what you have read in Chapters 29 to 31. Write your answers on a separate sheet of paper.

1. The people named below contributed to the pride that many Americans felt in the United States as it turned one hundred years old. Tell who each person was, and explained how he or she contributed to American pride.
   a. Mrs. E.D. Gillespie
   b. George Henry Corliss
   c. Alexander Graham Bell
   d. Elizabeth Cady Stanton
   e. Walter Camp
   f. Thomas Alva Edison
   g. Grosvenor Porter Lowrey

2. Imagine that you are writing an article called "Signs of Progress" about the United States at the end of the 1800s. Why would you describe each of these places in your article?
   a. Philadelphia
   b. Menlo Park
   c. New York City

3. Define each of these terms. Then explain its significance to the events of the times.
   a. centennial
   b. exposition
   c. consent of the governed
   d. exports
   e. middle class
   f. filament

4. Put yourself in the shoes of President Grant. You must write a brief speech for the opening ceremonies at the Centennial Exposition. What will you say about the state of the nation in 1876?

5. If you could visit the Centennial, which attraction would you want to see most? Why?

6. Some people in the nineteenth century described the rich and the poor as "two nations." What do you think they meant by this remark?

7. The first news of the battle of Little Bighorn reached eastern newspapers on July 5, 1876. This was smack in the middle of the Centennial Exposition. Create a mock dialogue between two fairgoers who have just learned about the defeat of George Armstrong Custer.

8. Thomas Alva Edison recruited some of the nation's most talented inventors to work at Menlo Park. Write a help-wanted ad that Edison might have written for a new assistant.

9. Thomas Edison said: "Genius is ninety-nine percent perspiration and one percent inspiration." What do you think he meant? Do you agree? Why or why not?

10. *Thinking about the Big Ideas:* A magazine reporter who visited Philadelphia in 1876 wrote: "The thousands who move among the Centennial marvels . . . wonder how their poor forefathers [and foremothers] lived a hundred years ago." What changes had taken place to make Americans think about this question?

Study Guide

PART 7

The Unfinished Journey (Chapters 32–37)

Answering the following questions will help you understand and remember what you have read in Chapters 32 to 37. Write your answers on a separate sheet of paper.

1. The people below played a key role in the lives of African Americans in the closing years of the nineteenth century. Tell who each person was, and explain how he or she took a stand on civil rights.
   a. Homer Plessy
   b. John M. Harlan
   c. Ida B. Wells
   d. Booker T. Washington
   e. W.E.B. DuBois

2. Suppose you are putting together a guide book entitled *African American Historical Landmarks in the United States.* Why might you include each of these places in your book?
   a. Holly Springs, Mississippi
   b. Hampton, Virginia
   c. Tuskegee, Alabama
   d. Great Barrington, Massachusetts
   e. Niagara Falls

3. Define each of the following terms. Then tell how each pair is linked.
   a. segregation, Jim Crow
   b. Redeemers, black codes
   c. voter fraud, poll tax
   d. white supremacy, Holocaust
   e. separate but equal, *Plessy* v. *Ferguson*
   f. vigilante justice, lynching

4. After Mark Twain read *Southern Horrors,* by Ida B. Wells, he wrote an essay entitled "The United States of Lynchdom." Pretend you are Twain. Write your own opening paragraph for his essay protesting mob murders.

5. Imagine you are one of the students at Tuskegee Institute. Both Booker T. Washington and George Washington Carver are among your teachers. Write a letter to a friend describing your studies.

6. The author named the chapter on Booker T. Washington "A Man and His Times." Why do you think she chose this title?

7. The author named the chapter on W.E.B. DuBois "A Man Ahead of His Times." Why do you think she chose this title?

8. Booker T. Washington wrote: "No race can prosper till it learns that there is as much dignity in tilling fields as in writing a poem. It is at the bottom of life that we must begin, and not at the top." How might W.E.B. DuBois react to this statement?

9. *Thinking about the Big Ideas:* Reread the dissenting, or minority, opinion of Justice John Marshall Harlan in the *Plessy* v. *Ferguson* case. How would Justice Harlan define the term *justice?*

10. *Thinking about the Big Ideas:* If you were an African American in the late 1800s, what changes would have to be made so that your children could enjoy the promise of equal justice for all?